Open My Heart, Lord

Healing for the Brokenhearted

Kathi Oates
& Robert Paul Lamb

Open Heaven Publications
P.O. Box 457/Moravian Falls, NC 28654
336-667-2333

Second Printing—January 2008

Open My Heart, Lord

ISBN 0-9752622-1-1

Requests for information should be directed to:

Open Heaven Publications
P.O. Box 457/Moravian Falls, NC 28654
336-667-2333

Printed in the United States of America

Dedication

To my Mother

Who became my best friend and confidante. Your nurturing has helped me through many rough times.

This book is for you, Mom.

Mary Ann Kelly
(1929-2006)

The Spirit of the Lord God is upon Me, because the Lord has anointed Me to bring good news to the afflicted; He has sent Me to bind up the broken-hearted, to proclaim liberty to captives, and freedom to prisoners.

Isaiah 61:1

Special Notice

Nothing in this book guarantees any specific result or outcome. The principles outlined herein are not a substitute for therapy. Persons who display dissociative symptoms are encouraged to seek the help of a competent Christian mental health professional trained in the fields of dissociation and trauma.

All testimonies presented in this book are true and accurate as presented. The names of the specific individuals are withheld for personal privacy reasons.

Table of Contents

Endorsements

A heart that is healed and free is desperately needed in the Body of Christ today. Too many Christians, even leaders, are trying to get the speck out of their brother's eye without noticing the beam in their own.

Kathi has ministered to me and our leadership team in Toronto, helping us to "see more clearly" and therefore be more effective in life and ministry. Her insights in this book will speed you on your way to healing, freedom and fruitfulness.

Carol Arnott, Founding Pastor
Toronto Airport Christian Fellowship

The dreams that we often hear described from the pulpits of the land will never be realized without us first learning how to live in victory over our past. Kathi Oates' book, *Open My Heart, Lord*, will guide great numbers of people to personal freedom, and ultimately on to their destiny.

She takes the reader from the theory of the classroom to the trenches of daily living. Her story of liberty can become your personal experience through studying this book.

Bill Johnson, Senior Pastor
Bethel Church, Redding, CA
Author, *When Heaven Invades Earth*

Healing the brokenhearted is a major key in receiving the new anointing that is being poured out on planet Earth.

Kathi teaches and has a special anointing on her prayer in the CD enclosed in the book to bring the shattered pieces of your heart back together.

Sid Roth, TV Host
It's Supernatural
Brunswick, GA

Though I am now in my 57th year of ordained ministry I can say without hesitation that God has used Gary and Kathi Oates to reveal truth to me I have not known before.

Kathi's book, *Open My Heart, Lord,* is confirmation of that statement. The Holy Spirit's incredible revelation through them is part of His end-times equipping for the Church.

The effect this book will have on your life parallels the day of the Resurrection when Jesus joined the disciples on the Emmaus road. After-wards, they said: *"Did not our hearts burn within us while He talked to us ..."* (Luke 24:31,32).

My prediction is this: You cannot read this book without burning in its power. More importantly, that "burning" will ignite those to whom you minister.

Charles Carrin
Author
The Edge of Glory

While Gary and Kathi were traveling with me on International trips in South America and Europe I became aware of a method of ministry Kathi was using that was helping people receive not only emotional healing, but often the emotional healing brought with it a physical healing.

Eventually, I had the opportunity to watch Kathi minister to a large group of people at a conference in Toronto, and heard of private ministry to some of the church's staff. The reports again were very positive. Her book, *Open My Heart, Lord*, was a very helpful book to understand the principles that were the basis for her practice of ministry to the brokenhearted which produced freedom for the captives.

I found the appendix also to be very helpful in understanding the conceptual basis for the model of ministry that has proven effective for ministering to people with varying degrees of dissociation.

The late John Wimber used to teach us that to play a good game of golf you needed more than a putter or driver, you needed the whole set of golf clubs. Kathi has given us another club to put in our bag of ministry. One that would not be appropriate for everyone, but very appropriate for some. I found the book very interesting. I think you will also.

Randy Clark,
Founder of Global Awakening
Harrisburg, Pennsylvania

Only a person who has experienced what Kathi Oates has gone through could have written a book like *Open My Heart, Lord.*

Only a person like Kathi Oates, who has attained a level of expertise through retrospective under-standing, divine revelation and an eye on the supernatural power of God, could have written as helpful a book as *Open My Heart, Lord.*

Only a person like Kathi Oates, who has been plunged into hand-to-hand combat and eyeball to eyeball ministry facing these issues all over the world, could have presented us with such a helpful book as this.

It will help anyone and everyone who reads it. It will transform many who allow its truths to pervade their souls and it will absolutely stand as a life and death matter in the lives of some.

I believe the material has come to Kathi from the heart of God. It has come to us from a heart that has sought God, has found Him and is seeking more.

Thanks, Kathi!

Jack R. Taylor
Dimensions Ministries
Melbourne, Florida

Preface

One of the overpowering things that has disturbed me for years is the huge numbers of wounded, broken and hurting people who sit in the average church Sunday after Sunday.

As a minister I have often reached out to bring the healing virtue of Jesus to many of these wounded saints. Often times, people turned upon me and attacked the one offering God's healing.

I have seen churches fail to progress in the plan of God because of wounded people in the core of their leadership or even worse, wounded warriors standing in the pulpit.

It is a tragedy that should never be.

Kathi Oates—exposing the pain of her past and the freedom of her present—now comes and tells us there is an answer in God. Her husband, Gary calls her sessions in their meetings (in the USA and abroad) the *most* important because she provides the keys to opening the supernatural realm.

There is healing for the affliction of your broken heart. There is an answer for the pain and suffering of your past. There is a way in God to walk in victory and Kathi's understanding brings that liberating truth to us in these pages.

That simple truth is this: Jesus Christ suffered on the Cross so that you would not have to continually bear the pain of your brokenness. The Savior not only took care of our eternity through His sacrificial death, but He also provided healing *now* for anyone that would suffer in being brokenhearted.

Hopefully, this book is about making that great biblical truth *experientially* real in the lives of all who will read these words. That is our heartfelt prayer before our Heavenly Father as we send this book forth.

Robert Paul Lamb
Co-author

Introduction

When Saul was selected as king of Israel (1 Samuel 10:1), the prophet Samuel took a flask of oil, poured it on his head, kissed him and said, *"Has not the Lord anointed you a ruler over His inheritance?"*

A short time later at Mizpah, Samuel called the people together to publicly confirm Saul's kingship so that both the people and Saul would have assurance of God's choice.

Saul, the son of Kish, was from the Matrite family of the tribe of Benjamin, the smallest of Israel's twelve tribes. So, this insecure man with a poor self-image from an insignificant family was called to become the king of Israel.

Yet, when he was supposed to be brought forth to be presented to the people, Saul could not be found. The Lord had to give instructions about Saul's location because he was hiding with the baggage.

He actually was curled up, cowering beside the baggage afraid to come into the destiny God had for him. Although God's anointing was upon him as king, this tall man in stature was controlled by self-doubt and fear—dominant forces in his life that were never healed.

In comparison with David, the Bible tells us something completely different about him as he went to battle with Goliath. He *"left his baggage in the care of the baggage keeper"* and *"ran to the battle line"* (1 Samuel 17:22). When confronted with an over nine-foot tall Goliath spewing curses and threats, *"David ran quickly toward the battle line to meet the Philistine"*(verse 48).

What a contrast!

Saul tried to face the challenges of life in his own strength (which he knew was inadequate), while David's confidence was in the Lord who had delivered him *"from the paw of the lion and from the paw of the bear"* (1 Samuel 17:37).

Saul is fairly typical of many of us. When faced with the call of God upon our lives and the opening of God's destiny, we somehow want to hide behind our baggage. Regrettably, some of the baggage is stuff we've carried around for years and it's designed to defeat us from God's great purpose in this life.

Because of certain painful events in our lives, many of God's precious people have built inner barriers or walls for protection. These are security blankets or defense mechanisms.

Most likely you are one of these people. You may be mad at God because He didn't answer your prayer. You expected God to do something and He didn't. Maybe you feel God let you down. It's hard to be intimate with someone you're mad at.

At times, events in our lives cause us to add new blocks to the walls already erected. Traumatic experiences happen, and people are often hurt or wounded.

Maybe you got hurt by a pastor or someone in ministerial authority. Perhaps you are disillusioned with the church. For others, it could have been a problem with a father or other authority figure.

We typically see God as being like our natural fathers. Could your image of your heavenly Father be flawed because of a poor relationship with your earthly father?

After a while, these inner walls become a protection for us. It allows us to keep functioning to avoid getting hurt again and again.

A woman came forward for prayer in one of our meetings and had a long list of problems to confront. "I've known the Lord for a long time and I love Him...but I'm just somehow not in touch with Him," she said dejectedly. "I can't see Him, feel Him or hear Him. It seems like He's nowhere in my life."

"Okay, let's take a moment here," I suggested. "I want you to ask God to reveal to you what these walls are in your life." I gave her a few words of instruction and then she prayed.

After a long pause, she then began repeating a list of "walls" as God was revealing them to her: abandonment, rejection, abuse and hurts of every kind imaginable.

"Those walls have been a protection to you," I explained. "They've become a friend seemingly protecting you from more hurt and pain, but they are keeping God out."

She nodded her head. "Are you willing to ask Jesus to deal with the walls and for Him to become that wall of protection for you, instead?" I asked.

She thought for a moment, and then slowly said "yes." She repeated a simple prayer and asked the Lord to come and minister to the walls. Tears began streaming down her face as we waited on the Lord.

"What's happening?" I questioned.

"Jesus is tearing the walls down," she answered. "He's destroying them. The walls are crumbling."

By now, she was weeping profusely. "What's happening now?" I asked.

"Jesus is coming towards me," she replied, "and He's telling me that He loves me...He's reaching out, holding me and hugging me."

In matter of minutes she went from not being "in touch" with God to a place of seeing, hearing and feeling His Presence. It was remarkable.

The woman was completely set free as Jesus removed the walls. The barriers and obstacles fell as we prayed together. When the obstructions in our lives—no matter what we call them—are removed, I believe intimacy with God follows.

Kathi and I took the Myers-Briggs test early in our marriage and scored at the opposite ends of the spectrum. Of course, we didn't need to take a test to make that discovery.

We seemingly had a way of arguing about everything. We hardly agreed on much of anything, and this was especially true during the days we pastored five different churches.

We'd go to church arguing all the way there. Naturally, at church, we'd put on a "smiley" face and speak the Christian language. Afterwards, we'd get in the car and argue all the way back home. It got so bad we ultimately had to travel in two cars. That went on for years.

In many ways we had been like Lazarus after he had been raised from the dead and walked out of the tomb. He was still bound hand and foot with grave clothes, and Jesus had to instruct His followers, *"Unbind him, and let him go,"* (John 11:44).

I was alive but bound just like Lazarus because I was carrying all of my baggage with me. In the case of the Oates' family, we may have looked fine outwardly, but inwardly, it was a different story.

Of course, Kathi thought all the problems were me and I naturally believed just the opposite was true. I blamed her for anything that went wrong in the church or the family. It was always her fault.

What a dilemma!

One day Kathi told me she was tired of blaming me for everything and had determined she was going to get some help. "Whether you do or not," she added.

Yet, Kathi's decision forced me to say, "I'm going to get help too—whether you do or not."

We found a licensed Christian counselor, Andrew Miller, who was able to get us focused in on the Lord to where we could hear what He wanted to heal inside of us. What followed was two full years of ministry that caused us to deal with issues and uncover all kinds of hidden conflicts (and belief systems) that were keeping us bound.

We are not talking about behavior modification, which can work—but only to a certain extent. God can show us the root cause of what is troubling each of us—and He alone knows. The healing of the deep wounds is what enabled us to lay the axe to the root of some problems, as well as to cut off some branches of wrong behavior. Healing flowed into our lives.

Along the way, I have discovered that the more healing I receive, the closer my relationship with the Lord becomes. Ultimately, greater anointing manifested in my life and broader usefulness in God's kingdom resulted. Improved healthy relationships with others also came.

We're all in a heavenly process—a process of being healed from those things which will hold us back from fulfilling our destiny as children of God. We haven't arrived yet, but—Praise God—we're headed in the right direction.

We still have our little disagreements but they are short-lived, and we are able to work right through them. In the past, it might have been a conflict lasting three or four days, but now we get focused on the *real* cause and move on.

The living God has healing and great usefulness available for all of us, and that is the wonderful truth behind this book.

This material represents keys to opening up the supernatural realm. When we allow the Lord to reveal the baggage in our lives and heal us in those areas, we will begin to experience more of the fullness of the Holy Spirit.

The anointing of God will be greater than you have ever known. You will be freer to function in healthy relationships with others. The gifts of the Spirit will manifest in a greater dimension and you will receive more revelation from God. Your prayer life will become much more effective as you are able to hear from God and pray about those things He reveals to you.

Read and receive your healing—then, begin to experience a new supernatural realm in your life.

Gary Oates, Author
Open My Eyes, Lord

Chapter 1

A Quest To Get Free

"...I have sought you all your life. Through all the pain, through all the loneliness, I have sought you. Each time your heart broke soundlessly with the agony of not belonging, I sought you. I was there, loving you. Reaching out to you. It was Me all along."

—from *Journal of the Unknown Prophet* by Wendy Alec

I grew up in a family that was co-dependent. By that, I mean there were a lot of control issues in the family, as well as alcoholism and a high degree of anger.

My dad came out of a background where he was basically raised by his mother. His own father was mostly "in and out" of the home, or an absentee parent in his rearing. By the time my dad was thirteen, he was forced into work in the steel mills to help his family survive the Depression griping the country at that time.

With the pressure and responsibility of a family (I was the oldest of four sisters) and a strong desire to succeed, my dad had a lot of pent-up anger and that anger would be directed at anyone he perceived was in his way.

He was verbally abusive to my mother and that created an atmosphere in the home where my sisters and I were disciplined in anger out of our parents' inflamed emotions. Perhaps, to some degree, that was typical of the 1950s culture where discipline was often administered to children with extreme spankings with a leather belt accompanied, by yelling and screaming.

In spite of that kind of climate at home, I experienced intermittent love and was very much doted on the first five years of my life. My parents meant well, but many times anger ruled.

Then, I entered a school situation where I was "a small fish in a big pond." I was simply overwhelmed.

My family was poor and we lived outside of town in the country. I dressed according to our meager finances. Also, I ate whatever came from the school lunchroom where my grandmother worked and it was mostly high starchy foods.

With the rejection at school and an unhealthy emotional situation at home, I turned to food as a cure for the feelings of emptiness and rejection I was experiencing on the inside. That created a cycle of more eating, getting fatter, and then experiencing more rejection.

By the time I reached the middle school years, I couldn't walk in a classroom without being teased, or snickered at. I was constantly being made fun of because I was so overweight. Yet, the more pain I felt, the more I ate.

Kids can be terribly brutal to one another. I was scared most of the time because I never knew when something bad was going to happen to me.

I never knew when I was going to be ridiculed, made fun of, or suffer extreme embarrassment over something. For instance, there were days I'd walk into class hearing the kids saying, "Fatty, fatty, two by four...can't get through the schoolhouse door!"

One day our bus slid off the road and into a ditch as we traveled home from school. I happened to be sitting on the side that landed in the ditch. For sometime afterwards, the kids all teased me that I was the reason the bus landed in the ditch.

It was horrible, and that kind of treatment traumatizes a child. I have often thought what seems like a minor thing to an adult can be very traumatic for a child, especially one who is as sensitive as I was.

When high school finally arrived, I had lived with "Fat Kathi" a long time. We were well acquainted.

But something had also happened in my life. My family had moved from a town in Alabama back to my home town in Ohio. During the move, I was so busy I didn't eat for three days and immediately lost ten pounds.

This started me on the track of losing weight and I began to research nutrition and good eating habits. As time passed, I became stricter with myself and began taking off enormous amounts of weight.

At sixteen I became a cheerleader in high school and began dating a guy from a neighboring town who was captain of the football team. I was finally living the life I had only dreamed about.

Regrettably (always fearing rejection), I was so insecure I couldn't keep a lasting relationship with anyone. I had few girl friends, but a long string of boy friends. Yet, I was accepted because I had become physically attractive and wanted to please whoever I was with.

As "Fat Kathi," I had received my affirmation from being a straight A student. Yet, when I lost weight I also began to lay aside everything that represented "Fat Kathi." I left the past and the person I had been behind me, and changed into a totally different person.

I didn't have a history of long-standing relationships with anybody. The minute I saw a flaw of any kind in them, I'd drop them.

But at the age of twenty, the Lord set me up. I met and married Gary Oates, the man of my dreams, in a brief three weeks. I certainly don't recommend that kind of quick courtship for anyone, but it was how the Lord worked with me.

After Gary and I were married, we spent more than thirty years pioneering new churches (which can be a very thankless task). We faced many challenges going into areas and starting churches from scratch.

We lived by faith—which meant we had no steady paycheck and had to trust God for everything. That seemingly always created pressure and stress.

I was a young pastor's wife in Gatlinburg, Tennessee when the Lord exploded our church with miracles happening in people's lives. People from the drug culture were frequently being converted.

Yet, in the midst of all that God was doing, I felt a high level of anger interacting with my two young daughters and trying to be a pastor's wife. Anger always involves some measure of control, and anger was a huge issue in our home.

I would gain the victory for awhile and then an unexpected situation would come out of nowhere, "triggering" the anger smoldering that was forever underneath the surface.

We had many "big name" speakers coming to the church and I often asked, "How do you get rid of your anger?"

The only thing they could offer was to "unload your plate." In other words, don't try to do so much. That was the wisdom of the day, but it never seemed to get to the real problem of why I had the anger in the first place.

I often struggled with simply keeping a lid on my anger because, at times, I felt I was about to "lose it"—and I really didn't know what I was dealing with.

In time I began to realize something was blocking me. Some unknown or unseen force was preventing me from experiencing most of God's promises of peace, joy, and happiness.

I was tired all the time—very, very tired. Pioneering a new church (which the late John Wimber often said takes 80 hours a week) and raising two active daughters left me physically and emotionally drained most of the time.

Much of my energy, it seemed, went towards keeping my anger under control. It takes a lot of energy to keep yourself in control when *inside* you are out of control.

By this time, the years of rejection (which is common in ministry) and rejection as a child were now piling up on the inside of me. I also found myself trying to please everybody because I didn't want them to reject me anymore. I did my best to do pleasing things to make people like me and want to come back to church. For a person with issues like mine, pioneering churches is a bad idea.

Somehow I always found myself trying to make sure that everyone was taken care of—having people over for dinners, Christmas, Thanksgiving, special occasions—where I cooked everything. I served my family the same way. I just couldn't stand for anybody but me to serve. In effect, that set me up to be everybody's caretaker.

I couldn't—or I should say *wouldn't*—allow my

two daughters to experience pain. I had to work tirelessly to keep that from happening.

For a time I thought the church or the ministry was my problem. Then, I became convinced my husband was the problem. But the Lord ultimately showed me the problem wasn't Gary, or the ministry. The problem was me. I was the one who needed to change.

Kathi Oates was the problem.

In time, the Lord began to show me I was full of pride and anger. Some of the answers came when we participated in a conference in Oregon where the power of God was present in a miraculous way. A little girl, deaf from birth, was standing in front of me and was totally healed by the power of God.

Even though we had been involved in powerful meetings in the past, I saw more power present in those meetings than ever before. I was prayed for and was knocked to the floor by some of that power.

Yet, when I came out of that meeting, the next emotion I experienced was anger. It was a constant underlying anger—always with me. No matter what I did it was always there.

I asked myself: why am I leaving a meeting with so much anger when I have experienced the power of God in my life? What's wrong with this picture?

I *knew* a genuine healing from God was possible—and I needed some deep, deep, deep healing in my life. I began to seek the Lord as never before. It was also the time I went to Gary saying, "I don't know what you're going to do but I'm going to get healing."

I never doubted the Lord wanted a people who were so full of the Holy Spirit that when they walked in the room the whole atmosphere of the room changed—and I was determined to be a person filled with the Holy Spirit to that degree.

Of course, I knew that would happen not because of anything those people (or I) did, but because of the One we are connected with—the Lord of all glory—Who *"for freedom...set us free..."* (Galatians 5:1).

I realized it was not about me keeping control of my behavior. It was about getting to the root of where that behavior began and being healed. As a believer I was not meant to live under the tyranny of anger, pain or fear. Healing was and is my right and privilege in Christ.

So I determined to go on a quest—a quest to get free. I didn't know where it would take me or what I would have to do. I simply knew I had to get free. Free from my anger. Free from my past. Free from my rejection. Free from whatever was dogging my path.

Where the journey would take me I did not know. I simply knew I had to begin.

Chapter 2

Works of the Flesh

"The heart is deceitful above all things, and it is exceedingly perverse and corrupt and severely, mortally sick! Who can know it [perceive, understand, be acquainted with his own heart and mind]?"

—Jeremiah 17:9 (Amplified Bible)

As I began my quest to get free, I realized that, obviously, the Lord would need to do some deep work within my innermost being. Then one day, I came across Proverbs 4:23 (NKJV).

Keep your heart with all diligence, for out of it spring the issues of life.

That verse told me I was dealing with some heart issues in my life. The anger I was confronting wasn't just a matter of dealing with an unpleasant problem I was facing. I created an atmosphere around me that was the result of something in my heart.

The Amplified Bible says, *"Keep and guard your heart with all vigilance and above all that you guard, for out of it flow the springs of life."* That means each of us have to set a diligent guard over what's going on in our hearts—for out of your heart flows the central issues of life.

The word "heart" in Hebrew is *leb*, which encompasses both the physical organ and a person's inner feelings and deepest thoughts. In a literal sense, it can be considered "the seat of the emotions."

Thus, whatever your emotions are sitting on or working from in your life—that little platform is your heart. Sometimes the word for heart can be interchangeably used with the word for Spirit which is *ruach* in Hebrew and *pneuma* in Greek.

Often times we don't realize it, but we are reflecting outwardly the struggles of our inner life.

For instance, if you are laboring out of fear, you will almost always create a negative environment of fear within your family.

Satan's tactics are fearful. Romans 8:15 connects fear *"to a spirit of slavery,"* which obviously ties us to the emotionally destructive influence of his (satan's) kingdom. If you are full of fear, anxiety, panic, dread, dismay, or worry, you are functioning under the influence of the wrong kingdom.

You may be in the midst of making an important decision for your life. It can be something that's a good idea. Unfortunately, if we are being driven or influenced by fear, we are not functioning in the love or peace of God, *"...because fear involves torment..."* (1 John 4:18, NKJV).

And *that* is not the basis for making any wise decision.

Life & Death Words

Our spoken words serve as containers for that which is in our heart. Proverbs 18:21 says *"Death and life are in the power of the tongue, and those who love it will eat its fruit."*

Words flowing out of our hearts are, literally, spiritual containers. These words can produce the substance of life or they can produce the substance of death.

Listen to Proverbs 15:4 (NKJV): *"A wholesome tongue is a tree of life, but perverseness in it breaks the spirit."*

The scribes and the Pharisees are a prime example of this life and death principle. They spoke religious words and phrases that originated with God in the beginning. But these Jewish leaders had a wrong spirit also flowing out of their heart. Thus, their words produced death.

The same is true in a family or a ministry. If the words we speak are based on fear or anger, they will produce death.

Conversely, if they are spoken from a basis of faith, the words will produce life in the hearers and life in their circumstances. Jesus proved this point countless times. *"It is the Spirit who gives life; the flesh profits nothing; the words that I have spoken to you are spirit and are life,"* John 6:63).

33

I saw this principle at work in my two daughters who were raised in a Christian home, attended Christian schools and knew biblical truths. But my heart had anger, unresolved pain, fear and insecurity. Thus, the container of my heart was contaminated in many ways because of the fear lying beneath the surface of my life.

Because I often spoke the right words with the *wrong* spirit, my two daughters also became angry, fearful and insecure. In time they had to seek healing as a result of my actions.

I also felt I had to control my daughters to keep them on the "straight and narrow" path. That led me to another discovery: where fear is involved, control and anger are also present.

Those negative influences seem to swirl around each other. If fear, anger and control are in our heart because of unresolved pain, then we create that whole atmosphere wherever we go. It also exposes the fact we are not trusting God as we should.

God wants to heal us so that we are functioning out of His heart. When we do, we have great peace with God and develop confidence in Him to solve any dilemma in our lives.

Deeds of the Flesh

In Galatians 5, the Scripture describes the fifteen *"deeds of the flesh"* (verses 19-21), which are *"immorality, impurity, sensuality, idolatry, sorcery, enmities, strife, jealousy, outbursts of anger, disputes, dissensions,   factions,   envying,   drunkenness, carousing..."*

These deeds of the flesh have also been referred to as, *"deeds of an uncircumcised heart."* Circumcision, of course, is the removal of the foreskin. It represents the removal of things negative and unnecessary.   I call them "old systems" that were set up to protect us.

God wants to do a work of circumcision in our hearts, which is, in essence, what sanctification is all about. This "cutting away," or circumcision can be an exceedingly painful process, like any major surgery, but God has made provision for our healing in this way.

The apostle Paul refers to this heart process in Romans 2:29, *"But he is a Jew who is one inwardly; and circumcision is that which is of the heart, by the Spirit, not by the letter..."*

The Amplified Bible expresses this verse in the following way:

> *But he is a Jew who is one inwardly, and [true] circumcision is of the heart, a spiritual and not a literal [matter]...*

Obviously there is a whole different work of the Holy Spirit involved in this circumcision of the heart. In fact, the Amplified Bible calls the fruit of the Holy Spirit *"the work which His presence <u>within</u> accomplishes..."* (Galatians 5:23, author's emphasis).

There is little question the Holy Spirit works

through us to advance the Kingdom of God. But we might conclude from these verses that the Holy Spirit's greatest work is *within* us—an interior work—truly a circumcision of the heart.

We must be freed from these deeds of the flesh and allow healing to come to those needed areas of our hearts if we are ever to become the vessels God intended. The list of these "works of the flesh" or "deeds of an uncircumcised heart" is most revealing.

The Message Bible describes these practices of the flesh in an unvarnished, blistering and descriptive contemporary language. It is language that speaks directly to the heart of the matter:

> ...repetitive, loveless, cheap sex; a stinking accumulation of mental and emotional garbage; frenzied and joyless grabs for happiness; trinket gods; magic-show religion; paranoid lone-liness; cutthroat competition; all-consuming-yet-never-satisfied wants; a brutal temper; an impotence to love or be loved; divided homes and divided lives; small-minded and lopsided pursuits; the vicious habit of deper-sonalizing everyone into a rival; uncontrolled and uncontrollable addict-ions; ugly parodies of community...

In a certain sense these fifteen separate "works" or "deeds" of transgression (according to the *New American Standard Bible*) can be categorized into four distinct areas.

Works of the Flesh

Sexual

The first three in the Galatians 5 listing—immorality, impurity, sensuality—can be classified all in the sexual area. Please note that the King James Version of the Bible lists four "works" or "deeds" (instead of three) as adultery, fornication, uncleanness, and lasciviousness.

In many countries there is little difference between the morality of the church and the morality of the world. Some young people believe it's okay to live together and not be married. Yet, they go to church on Sundays.

1 Corinthians 6:18 exhorts mankind: *"Flee immorality. Every other sin that a man commits is outside the body, but the immoral man sins against his own body."*

That's why God is against sin. It destroys and it primarily hurts the person living in that lifestyle. People unfortunately justify their actions and think it's okay. However, <u>destruction will follow</u>. The Bible is clear about that.

This includes sexual addictions that have to do with sight such as pornography, or with touch, such as masturbation. These addictions are sinful because they are characterized by destructive thoughts and behavior, such as lust. All sin is destructive in nature.

Anything in our lives—*anything*—that produces death or destruction is sin. It can even look good from a religious perspective but if it produces destruction, it is sin. The issue is that plain.

The Amplified Bible provides us with an arresting definition of sin in 1 John 3:4:

> *Everyone who commits (practices) sin is guilty of lawlessness; for [that is what] sin is, lawlessness (the breaking, violation of God's law by transgression or neglect—being unrestrained and unregulated by His commands and His will).*

Sin produces death and death comes from destructive behavior. Around the world, it would be difficult to find a more destructive set of behaviors than those surrounding sex. Sex with more than one partner, whether inside or outside of marriage, is a major factor in the transmission of disease and HIV/AIDS.

Those who have embraced an alternative lifestyle often find themselves in destructive relationships (emotionally or physically) that they cannot break away from. Unfortunately, these relationships often end in death by violence or disease. The current average life span for people who live or practice an alternative lifestyle (most often homosexual or lesbian) is about 45 years of age. This is tragic.

There is little question that many who embrace an abusive or alternative lifestyle are doing so because of hurts, wounds and festering problems that began in their childhood.

In addition, it is known that homosexual tendencies can be generational—that is, passed from one generation to the next. That is why many in these lifestyles feel "born that way."

Exodus 20:5 acknowledges that some sins are indeed generational being passed *"on the third and fourth generations."*

Yet, God our Father is offering us freedom and liberty. He bought it for us on the Cross. He wants to heal our brokenness and put us back together again in His divine order and beauty.

Superstition & Witchcraft

The next two in our "works" or "deeds"— idolatry and sorcery—could be connected to areas of superstition and witchcraft.

Idolatry (from the Greek *eidololatreia*) is basically defined as "image worship" and can include anything that our affections are passionate about. It can also involve extravagant admiration of the heart.

Colossians 3:5 says *"Therefore consider the members of your earthly body as dead to immorality, impurity, passion, evil desire, and greed, which amounts to idolatry."*

Idolatry can be anything we look to in order to sustain us in our personhood other than the Lord Jesus Christ. It is literally anything we serve as our master—other than Him!

Sorcery or witchcraft (from the Greek *pharmakeia*) originally described the use of medicine, drugs, or spells. Later it came to refer to sorcery, accompanied by drugs, incantations, charms, and magic. It is connected to the practice of dealing with evil spirits, and can be centered on magical incantations or casting spells upon someone by means of drugs or potions, but not necessarily.

Many would be horrified to consider that sorcery or witchcraft exists in Christian circles but it is true. Witchcraft is based on control, such as, "How can I control my circumstances or the people around me?"

Ministers learn how to manipulate and control people to get accomplished whatever that particular minister thinks ought to be done. This control is often exerted through guilt or carefully chosen means of overpowering or intimidating a person. Whatever the method, it is still a form of witchcraft.

Revelation 9:21 describes an apocalyptic scene involving mankind when the sixth trumpet of God sounds. *"And they did not repent of their murders nor of their sorceries nor of their sexual immorality nor of their thefts."*

Temperament

The next eight "works" or "deeds" of the flesh from Galatians 5 include enmities, strife, jealousy, outbursts of anger, disputes, dissensions, factions and envying. These could all be lumped into sins of temperament.

Works of the Flesh

Here again, the King James Version lists nine in this category: hatred, variance, emulations, wrath, strife, seditions, heresies, envying and murder.

Enmities or hatred (from the Greek *echthra*) is a bitter dislike, abhorrence or ill-will against anyone. It can also embrace holding a grudge against or being angry at someone.

This is a deed that can be located very deep in one's heart. Nobody sees hatred because we learn how to put on a pleasant face. The result is that the ugliness of what is truly in our heart is not very visible, if at all.

1 John 1:9, 11 describes the condition of a person who is bound by hatred. *"The one who is in the Light yet hates his brother is in the darkness until now...But the one who hates his brother is in the darkness and walks in the darkness, and does not know where he is going because the darkness has blinded his eyes."*

Strife (from the Greek *eritheia*) is a contentious dispute about words. It can also be a contest for superiority or advantage, and may involve paying someone back in kind for wrongs done.

In writing about his visit to the church at Corinth, the apostle Paul wonders about the condition of the congregation. *"For I am afraid that perhaps when I come I may find you to be not what I wish and may be found by you to be not what you wish; that perhaps there will be strife, jealousy, angry tempers, disputes, slanders, gossip, arrogance, disturbances,"* (2 Corinthians 12:20).

OPEN MY HEART, LORD

Jealousy or emulations (from the Greek *zeloi*) is defined as seeking to surpass and outdo others, striving to excel at the expense of another, or an uncurbed spirit of rivalry.

The Body of Christ is riddled with jealousy and envying (from the Greek *phthonoi*). It is particularly dangerous for leaders who are focused upon building MY church or MY ministry.

In Ezekiel 8:3, the Lord caught the prophet Ezekiel up by a lock of his head and brought him *"to Jerusalem, to the entrance of the north gate of the inner court, where the seat of the idol of jealousy, which provokes to jealousy, was located."*

This passage further explains this *"idol of jealousy"* keeps men from the Presence of God.

To observe some people in ministry, it appears to be all about using others or manipulating them to get whatever the person wants or thinks they need. Such an attitude unquestionably leads to jealousy that provokes men to jealousy.

It keeps people from the Presence of God, because the real deal is all about laying down my life so somebody else can go forward. It's all about being sure whatever I have gets multiplied so the Kingdom of God can be advanced.

I know a minister who personally funded a number of outdoor crusades in a country in South America. The final night before returning to the USA, the minister was due to preach. Instead, he gave up his spot to a young man who had an obvious anointing to reach a particular people group in that nation.

The minister coached the young man through the service and God brought great fruit with many being saved and healed. It was an investment in the young man's life but came at the sacrifice of the other man's ministry.

That kind of sacrifice should be the norm in the Body of Christ. Regrettably, in some ministry situations, it is all about "big" names. Instead, the goal of all ministers should be to raise up others so the Body of Christ is multiplied as new ministries step forward to meet the challenges of the 21st Century.

Outbursts of anger or wrath (from the Greek *thumos*) can involve determined, lasting anger where self-control is lost. The Amplified Bible calls it *"ill temper,"* but it can also embrace rage, turbulent passions, indignation, and fierceness.

Colossians 4:8 challenges us with these words. *"But now you also, put them all aside: anger, wrath, malice, slander, and abusive speech from your mouth."*

Outbursts of anger were one of the great strongholds in my life. I had to stand up and honestly declare, "This is a problem in my life."

Anger is one of the biggest protections employed by people. If someone steps on us or seeks to invade our space, we might flare up in anger creating a wall of protection around us.

OPEN MY HEART, LORD

Many times anger is used to control others, as well as cover up fear. Anger can be used to manipulate others with facial expressions and body language, or in the withdrawal of affection or attention. This is called passive/aggressive behavior.

Subtle ways of manipulating people can be more effective in controlling situations than outbursts of anger. Yet, they are both destructive.

Disputes, dissensions and factions are expressed by the Amplified Bible as *"selfishness, divisions (dissensions), party spirit (factions, sects with peculiar opinions, heresies)."*

New churches are often birthed out of a party spirit. People in dissension at one church go down the street and start another church based on their particular beliefs or opinions.

Sometimes, it involves nothing more than selfishness. The attitude of some is: "If I can't have MY way, I'll go somewhere else to do whatever I want." If these self-centered people aren't careful, they will ultimately give birth to doctrines based on heresy. One has only to look at church history to realize the truth of that statement.

These disputes, dissensions and factions often occur because we feel insecure about who we are. We don't feel secure enough in ourselves to be able to handle error in others and still love them. I have observed many relationships are often based on doctrine rather than loving people as our brothers and sisters in Christ.

Works of the Flesh

Appetite

The last two of the fifteen works of the flesh listed in Galatians 5 are drunkenness and carousing which can be connected to the sins of appetite or drunkenness itself.

Drunkenness (from the Greek *methai*) is defined as living intoxicated or becoming a slave to drink, while carousing (from the Greek *komoi*) centers upon revellings, rioting, or lascivious and boisterous feastings.

Drunkenness can also be characterized by enslavement to drugs—even prescription ones. The underlying cause, of course, is to anesthetize the deep pain in a person's heart.

In some cases, when a person has been delivered from alcohol or drugs, they can still carry great pain underneath the surface. Some pursue other activities to keep the pain in check. A few even throw themselves into ministry which can be highly addictive.

The issue is not simply being set free from alcohol or drug addictions. These are often only symptoms, surface behaviors masking deeper pain. The issue is about uncovering what's underneath. True freedom comes when one is cleaned up, on the outside and on the inside, from the pain and trauma hiding underneath.

During what has been called "a time of the healing evangelists," which lasted from the late 1940s through about 1960, God sovereignly

45

empowered and worked through a cadre of anointed men and women. Great healing miracles that rivaled the Book of Acts occurred with some of these individuals.

Unfortunately some of them—who had been greatly used of God to bring His healing message to that generation—ultimately lost their way through lifestyles that were touched by these sins of appetite or drunkenness.

In truth, many of these individuals had heart issues that had never been resolved, leaving them at the mercy of these sins of the flesh.

In Luke 21:34, Jesus warns us about our lifestyle in the last days. *"Be on guard, so that your hearts will not be weighted down with dissipation and drunkenness and the worries of life, and that day will not come on you suddenly like a trap."*

Chapter 3

Trauma

"None of us can escape the effects of spiritual warfare. We are all vulnerable, and the world fractures us in many ways throughout our lives. Consequently, we are unable to avoid traumas, some of which leave long lasting scars."

—from *Living from the Heart Jesus Gave You* by James Wilder et al.

Under the inspiration of the Holy Spirit, the writer of Proverbs penned these insightful words:

> *The spirit of man is the lamp of the Lord, searching the innermost parts of his being* (Proverbs 20:27).

The New King James Version expresses that verse as: *"The spirit of man is the lamp of the Lord searching the inner depths of his heart."* In a literal sense the Hebrew meaning here involves a searching of the "rooms of the belly." Obviously, there are many parts or "rooms" of our innermost being.

What does that verse really mean?

It means your spirit—the innermost part of

your being—has registered literally everything that has ever happened to you. Your spirit knows every thought you have ever had. Even in the womb, your spirit records your life.

If you doubt that statement, listen to the words of the apostle Paul, *"For who among men knows the thoughts of a man except the spirit of the man which is in him? Even so the thoughts of God* no one knows except the Spirit of God" (1 Corinthians 2:11).

Our spirit knows what has happened to us from conception to this very day. Proverbs 14:10 agrees: *"The heart knows its own bitterness, and a stranger does not share its joy."*

Your spirit knows the *real* truth of everything that has occurred in your life, and, of course, God knows the real truth. I live continually asking that question: "What is the real truth here?"

There are so many confusing situations that confront us in life. You can have two people functioning in a church setting (doing the same thing)—one is motivated out of love and another motivated out of selfish ambition. How do you know the difference?

Proverbs 16:2 says *"All the ways of a man are clean in his own sight, but the Lord weighs the motives."*

Some people are absolutely motivated by a selfish, religious spirit. That was certainly the case of Ananias and Sapphira, who sold a piece of property, lied to the Holy Spirit about the transaction, and lost their lives as a result (Acts 5:1-11).

Externally, it looked as if Ananias and Sapphira were giving just like everybody else, but Peter caught the larceny in their hearts. They were appearing outwardly to do one thing, but the truth was a completely different matter.

This kind of thing is commonplace when people appear outwardly to be doing something that is pleasing to God. Yet, inwardly it is a complete lie.

Others like Mary, one of the sisters of Lazarus, were genuinely motivated out of the love of God. At the risk of great conflict with the disciples, who viewed her actions as waste, she anointed Jesus with a pound of costly oil of spikenard and wiped his feet with her hair (John 12:2-8). Yet, her motive was simply love. She loved Jesus.

Brokenhearted

Seven hundred years before Jesus Christ came to earth, the prophet Isaiah spoke about the mission of God's Messiah.

> *The Spirit of the Lord God is upon Me, because the Lord has anointed Me to bring good news to the afflicted; He has sent Me to bind up the brokenhearted, to proclaim liberty to captives and freedom to prisoners* (Isaiah 61:1).

Although healing of the emotions is part of the

package, the primary emphasis for the Lord Jesus (God's Messiah) is healing of the brokenhearted, which includes healing of the emotions. Psalm 147:3 concurs: *"He heals the brokenhearted and binds up their wounds."*

The Scriptures teach two different types of being brokenhearted—one is a type of humbling where we give up our own way. That is a brokenness the Lord does not despise. In fact, He loves that kind of brokenness.

A Good Brokenness

We finally admit (after much struggle and failure) that we can't do it anymore. It's about Him doing it through us. That's a good brokenness. It's constructive because it gets us "in tune" with His kingdom.

David describes this kind of brokenness in Psalm 51 after being confronted by the prophet Nathan (2 Samuel 12) over his adultery with Bathsheba and the death of their "love" child.

In Psalm 51:6, David acknowledges what God wants in an individual's life. *"Behold, You desire truth in the innermost being, and in the hidden part You will make me know wisdom."*

It is evident that David was not functioning out of that kind of truth in his innermost being when he took another man's wife, committed adultery with her, impregnated her, and then had him (Bathsheba's husband, Uriah) killed in battle.

When David sinned and was caught, it broke his heart. Not just because he was caught, though. His heart broke because he saw the extent of his sinfulness. He was broken by the pain of all that he had done and he offered it as a sacrifice to God.

Out of his brokenness, David writes: *"Purify me with hyssop, and I shall be clean; wash me, and I shall be whiter than snow," (verse 7).*

Hyssop was an herb associated with cleansing and purification (Numbers 19:6). The Hebrew word for "wash" is not the one used for the simple cleaning of a pot in water, but rather the washing of clothes by beating and pounding. David was crying out for cleansing in his innermost being.

It is getting real before God, admitting what we did and that we cannot control ourselves. Therefore, we hand this brokenness to God as a sacrifice. He will not despise this kind of offering, according to Psalm 51:16-17.

> *For you do not delight in sacrifice, otherwise I would give it. You are not pleased with burnt offering.*
> *The sacrifices of God are a broken spirit; a broken and a contrite heart, O God, You will not despise.*

A Destructive Brokenness

On the other hand, there is a brokenness that is not healthy. It is destructive. That occurs when we have an emotional "break" in our lives and our heart holds the pain or the anger or the shame, and we leave it in that state—turned inwardly. We don't offer it as a sacrifice to God.

That kind of brokenness, the kind which stays inside of us, is referred to in Proverbs 17:22 where it says *"...a broken spirit dries up the bones."*

The writer of Proverbs makes an identical point in Proverbs 15:13. *"A glad heart makes a cheerful countenance, but by sorrow of heart the spirit is broken"* (Amplified).

I prayed for a woman in Ukraine who was afflicted with rheumatoid arthritis and could barely walk up to me in the prayer line. Afterwards, the pain of the arthritis left but came back the next day. This often occurs because we don't get to the root cause of why a person is experiencing certain physical ailments.

So I asked the Lord to take this woman where she needed to go on the inside and bring up whatever needed to be healed in her heart. She remembered feeling responsible for the death of a son when she was a young woman. She literally hated that part of herself.

The Lord began ministering to the woman that the child's death was not her fault and that her child was in heaven with Him. She realized that she had been holding onto shame and guilt over the death of this child.

As she began forgiving herself, she embraced that part of her heart (which is the binding up process). "I'm so sorry I left you back there to hold all the shame," she cried. "It wasn't your fault. I'm sorry I treated you that way. Come back and be a part of me. With the Lord's help, I will take care of you."

As she embraced that whole section of her heart from which she had been disengaged, the peace of God came upon her and the power of God manifested in her body. She fell to the floor. Later when she got up, virtually every bit of her arthritis was gone. She had experienced a mighty touch from the Lord.

Healing in Colombia

A brokenness that is turned inward will ultimately become destructive. Proverbs 18:14 asks this question: *"...as for a broken spirit who can bear it?"*

I have learned in ministering to people that when a person's countenance is sad, there is a broken spirit involved. That was the case of a woman in Colombia suffering from tuberculosis. In fact, this woman was contagious and probably should have not been in the meeting.

The woman had to be helped up to the prayer line and could not even stand for prayer. As the Lord began delivering her from a spirit of death, I asked Him to take her where she needed to go. She suddenly saw herself as a little girl being abused by her mother. She hated herself because she could not love what her mother seemingly despised.

The woman released her anger towards her mother, and asked the little girl to come back and be a part of her life. At that point, the peace of God came over her as the splintered parts of her heart were integrated. She fell to the floor for a time.

When she finally stood, she began walking under her own power. There was no more coughing and no visible signs of the tuberculosis. She walked off with the peace of God in her heart and a smile on her face.

Understanding Trauma

In the Hebrew language the word "broken" implies being struck by a heavy blow emotionally. *Webster's Dictionary* says broken means split or cracked into pieces, splintered, fractured or burst.

We frequently use the word "trauma" which means a bodily injury, wound, or shock. When used in psychiatry, it means a painful emotional experience or shock that often produces a lasting effect.

According to the book, *Living From the Heart Jesus Gave You*, traumas "are the wounds (or injuries) left in our identities that render us less than what God had in mind when He created us."

When we experience any kind of trauma, we react in an emotional way—either with anger, pain, shame, guilt, rejection, fear or terror. These emotions arise in response to what is being done with or against us. The emotions can become so strong that we don't have any place to process them. There is simply no place to put them.

Trauma

These emotions are so toxic that if we lived in them or felt them, we probably could not function because of the intense pain. Thus, a part of our heart breaks off to hold these emotions that came with the trauma. In essence, this becomes a part or a "stuffing place" for anything else that comes along in life like the original trauma.

"Trauma" can convey more than just being hit or struck. It can also mean "fracture" in the sense of a broken bone.

The word "wound"—which is tied to the words broken and trauma—encompasses any hurt or injury to a person's feelings or sense of honor.

Notice the words of David from Psalm 109:22, *"For I am afflicted and needy, and my heart is wounded within me," (author's emphasis).* The literal meaning in the underlined passage is that someone has pierced my heart within me.

These shattering events seem to occur when one least expects them. Sometimes they come with an overwhelming suddenness and seem to last for an eternity.

Extreme Trauma

An extreme trauma can come about through an abortion, rape, a death in the family (or even the death of a pet), an accident, a divorce, a molestation of a child, or a deep hurtful situation with your parents. With me, I experienced rejection through being overweight.

OPEN MY HEART, LORD

There is little question that a traumatic event can strike a person in their spirit and heart and fracture them into tiny parts that usually personify the age in which the trauma occurred.

Many times these parts not only appear as a little person, but as a part that holds a definite emotion like a "broken part", an "angry part" or a "shamed part". It all depends upon what the Lord brings up to the person during a time of ministry.

What God does in these ministry instances is usually pinpoint accurate and individually tailored. There is no "set pattern" that occurs.

Some people will envision Jesus going in and doing something with that broken part to alleviate the pain or destructive emotion. Then, that now-recovered part is brought back to their heart where genuine wholeness can occur.

Of course, wholeness is the goal here. That's what Jesus came to accomplish—to put us back together, bind up our brokenness and restore us to a God-ordained wholeness.

Molestation

If statistics are correct, there are people reading this book who have been molested as children. You may have lived with that darkness hovering over your life for years.

It may have happened only once with another child. It may have occurred over a longer period of time with a trusted relative or another adult who was

56

an authority figure in your life. But the painful truth is that it happened!

For instance, I worked with a young woman who was under psychiatric care because of a sleeping disorder. She was taking prescription medication which often did not work. She was also facing issues of great fear and uncontrollable anger in her life. Her only son was even talking of suicide.

She had initially received some healing during one of our mission trips. Yet, problems persisted and we scheduled an afternoon of prayer.

During that time, the Lord brought back some memories where she saw herself as a six-year-old ballerina who had been sexually abused by the grandfather of a friend. She had visited her friend's home and had a flashback of what happened in the family's basement. She also saw a room that was very evil and memory of a ritual abuse surfaced.

The trauma that was released from that childhood incident caused her to shake from virtually every muscle in her body for several minutes as she was freed from years of hidden torment.

As time passed, she pursued further inner healing with other therapists, revealing other molestations had occurred. I am pleased to report this woman is now able to sleep peacefully and has conquered most of her troubling anger problems. Her son is at peace as well.

Whether the molestation was ongoing or not,

it usually results in the victim feeling a lot of shame, fear and terror. They learn to hate a part of themselves thinking they are dirty, or the molestation was their fault.

These emotions of shame, fear, guilt and anger are held onto by the heart because the molestation was forced on the victim. Yet, they feel somehow responsible for whatever happened.

I have discovered, as part of the restoration process, that the Lord has to release the victim from this false sense of responsibility. And, He has to be the One who does it.

The victim also needs to experience a sense of cleansing from the molestation. During molestation, there is a mingling of spirits as well as a mingling of physical bodies.

1 Corinthians 6:16 conveys the image of becoming *"one body"* with whoever the sexual act is committed. In a sense, there is a oneness that occurs even in a case of molestation, and the molester's spirit needs to be broken off the victim.

Some might consider this a breaking of "soul ties" but I believe it is literally a pulling out of the molester's spirit. Such a ministry removes the residue from the victim's spirit and the control issues involved with the molestation.

I have prayed these prayers over traumatized wives in a variety of scenarios with abusive husbands. Sometimes the wives find it nearly impossible to break the abusive connection long after the marriage might have ended.

It is more than just an entangled emotional issue. Ties in the spirit dimension must be broken. Because the wives were "one flesh" with the husbands, they have to be released and cleansed. The same is true with victims of molestation.

God has brought an answer to each of us—no matter the circumstances of whatever has happened in our lives. There is healing, wholeness and freedom available for you.

Divorce & Rejection

In the case of a divorce, the child might struggle with the feeling the parent has abandoned them, or even feel that the divorce was *their* fault.

The child might possibly labor under the shame and guilt of a divorce. A part of the child's heart might break off and hold onto the pain of abandonment and separation.

When a child is accosted by an adult or an authority figure, it can be overwhelming to the child's sense of trust and security. The child can then begin to hate a part of themselves feeling as if they did something wrong.

Rejection can manifest in a variety of ways, either from parents, family members or classmates. A child can be angry about the mistreatment and mistakenly hold onto the pain and trauma.

I just recently prayed for a man who had

grown up in a small town where he was a star baseball player. He got a lot of accolades from sports and a lot of attention from people as to who he was. Then, his father's plant shut down and they had to move to a large city.

He had no emotional support from his parents with the trauma of the move. A part of his heart held onto the pain for many years as he wrestled with being unaccepted, rejected and alone.

Sometimes aloneness can be the worst trauma. At least with abuse, there is some kind of attention. Yet with aloneness, it is as if you don't even exist.

There must be a place to work through the pain of what has occurred in these agonizing situations. The pain has to go somewhere.

So, our heart breaks off and we dissociate or disengage from a part of who we are at the time of the trauma. That part then holds the pain. A part can be formed not only to hold pain but it can be formed to hold anger when anger is not acceptable. Most of us just stuff the anger and pain deep inside.

A Pastoral Testimony

Recently, I prayed with a man on the pastoral staff of a large church who had been suffering through some pain that began when he was six years old. As a pastor's son, he had been raised in Africa. Then, one day his parents decided to send him to a boarding school for a proper education and to help cure his "free spirit".

Trauma

The boarding school was rigid and rule oriented, and he became the bad boy because he couldn't sit still. He suffered painful beatings from the school master as well as rejection from his parents for being placed in the boarding school. He was constantly told that he was bad.

When I asked about any problem with anger, his answer was immediate. "No, I never feel anger," he said. His reply was such because a hidden part of his heart was holding all the anger.

When he finally got in touch with the anger, he was set free. I asked the Lord to remove all the anger, all the hatred, the resentment and bitterness from his heart. He asked that little boy of six to come back into his life.

The man was sabotaging himself in his work at a church. The problem stemmed from him not being totally whole and the person God made him to be. When he embraced that part of his heart, his life changed dramatically.

If you had to feel the intensity of the pain every day of your life, you would not be able to function at all. So, you just push it to the side. Even when a trauma occurs, the pain will get stored so we can function. We always move toward functioning.

Think of it like a broken leg. There are varying degrees of fractures. It could be a hairline crack or a total break with space between the displaced parts. The same is true of the traumas that happen in our lives.

You might ask yourself, how can some people actually be saved when they are so splintered and traumatized?

In truth, when you got saved, your spirit did not become perfect. You received a deposit of the kingdom of God and the DNA of the Father dropped into your spirit. Now the sanctification process starts and begins to do its work perfecting your spirit and your soul.

This sanctification process is meant to permeate every facet of your being.

Jesus said *"...the kingdom of heaven is like leaven..."* (Matthew 13:33). You throw it in a peck of meal; go away, return and it's permeated the whole peck of meal.

In another sense the kingdom is also like a mustard seed (Matthew 13:31-32). You drop mustard seeds in a field. When you come back it's filled the whole earth.

That's not only how the kingdom operates, it also is how the kingdom operates within you.

In 1 Thessalonians 5:23, the apostle Paul says *"...may the God of peace Himself sanctify you entirely; and may your spirit and soul and body be preserved complete."*

*Wuest's Translation of the New Testa*ment translates that verse as:

Now, may the God of peace Himself

consecrate you, every part of each one of you, to His worship and service, and your spirit and soul and body be preserved <u>in their entirety</u> blameless at the coming of our Lord Jesus Christ. (*emphasis added*)

Why would you have to include the word *"spirit"* in that Scripture if a person's spirit was already sanctified?

It is obvious that Paul is praying for his converts to be wholly sanctified, that is, that their whole being—spirit, soul, and body—might be yielded to the will of God.

In 2 Corinthians 7:1, Paul says that we must *"cleanse ourselves from all defilement of flesh and spirit..."* That raises a vital question. If your spirit is perfect, how can it become defiled?

There are many scriptures that go against a "perfect spirit" doctrine. Yet most of our westernized Christianity is based upon that teaching.

You are a spirit but you are also a soul. The word for spirit was interchangeable with soul in the Hebrew language. That's because they are so tightly intertwined they cannot be separated.

A Summary

Trauma is common to all of us. It is something so potent that it can break your heart and cause you to dissociate from the pain, the fear, and the anger.

OPEN MY HEART, LORD

It is possible we don't even know or understand what has happened to us with the trauma of our lives because we are so accustomed to operating with just part of ourselves instead of the whole.

The young woman (I mentioned earlier), who had suffered several instances of sexual abuse as a child, had no memory of those events until she felt safe enough the issues would be taken care of. Then the memory started to bleed over from the subconscious mind (or the depth of the spirit) into her conscious mind.

These were not memories that were suggested to her. They were memories that came from inside of her. There was never any suggestion that she had been the victim of any kind of molestation.

Yet, when she felt safe, the memories began to surface and the Lord began her healing process. Individuals usually must experience that sense of safety before genuine healing can take place.

In its purest form, salvation means to be delivered and made whole. I believe that happens through the process of sanctification and the healing of the brokenhearted.

Talking to the religious establishment of His day, Jesus warned *"You are of your father the devil, and you want to do the desires of your father...Whenever he speaks a lie, he speaks from his own nature, for he is a liar and the father of lies,"* (John 8:44)

Trauma

In essence, He was saying: you religious people don't know the *real* truth about yourselves.

The same could be said for many of us!

Many of us still operate out of what we think the truth is, not was it really is. God is the only One who knows the truth, and He sent the Holy Spirit to lead and guide us into all the truth.

We are such great masters at denial. And because of that, we honestly don't know ourselves. Therefore, we need to ask the Lord to show us where the traumas are in our lives.

Our conscious mind does not know the real truth of our lives, but our spirits do. This is where the work of the Holy Spirit becomes absolutely vital. He will facilitate whatever needs to be healed in our lives.

Chapter 4

Walls & Lies

"The mind interprets this (destructive) behavior as a solution to a problem, even when it risks ruining your life...It is a protective measure gone awry...The cure is figuring out what painful issue or event you are trying to protect yourself from facing."

—Dr. Gail Saltz as quoted in *Parade*, June 11, 2006

As the Lord began to heal various areas of my emotions—and even different memories—I began to experience a new freedom and liberty in my life. Then, a problem arose.

I had gone down alone to a pastors' conference in south Florida where a friend was speaking. While there, I was negatively affected by a certain pastor's wife. She seemed happy and content being a pastor's wife and I was not.

On the way back home I realized there was still a war on my insides. There was a whole part of me that I *really* hated.

A short time later our Tallahassee church held a conference with a man who ministered inner healing, and I had volunteered as his "guinea pig." He sat me down in front of the group and asked the Lord to take me where I needed to go inside myself.

The first thing the Lord brought up was false images of Jesus that had to be smashed. They were religious images and false belief systems I had about Jesus. Anyone who has been in the church for any length of time has a few of these.

I saw the Lord come and break those images in pieces.

Then I said, "I see a wall."

"What's the name of the wall?" he asked.

"Fear."

"Are you willing to have the Lord come and minister to that fear?" he inquired.

"Yes."

Once again, I saw the Lord come and take the fear. He smashed the wall and blew the pieces away. All of these images were vivid in my mind

Then he asked, "Is there anything behind the wall?"

"I see a little girl."

"What's her name?" he persisted.

"Fat Kathi."

"How does she feel?" he questioned.

"She feels very sad."

"Are you willing to go love on her?"

"No, I hate her," I said firmly.

He was quiet for a moment, and then asked, "Are you willing to have the Lord come minister to her?"

"Okay," I agreed. I saw the Lord come and put His arm around her. She appeared to feel less sad. As I looked at her, I thought, "I have lost a lot of who I am in her. I lost a lot of my intellect and my focus in her. She was such a vital part of who I was for at least ten years and I had just left her behind."

At the counselor's suggestion, I asked "Fat Kathi" to come be a part of me again. When I did, it was like two large pieces of a puzzle being slammed together again. The effect was so jarring I had to have Gary come and hold me.

Sometime later, I was still dealing with feelings of rejection, shame, and pain. So I contacted a counselor friend. He asked a simple question: "When you asked 'Fat Kathi' back, did you release any of the trauma that was in her?"

"No, I didn't."

"That's a step we have to take," he suggested.

Right there on the phone, we began praying

the Lord would take away all the anger, pain, shame and rejection over the way I looked as a child— emotions that "Fat Kathi" wrestled with. I could feel it leaving.

I began to get freer and freer and freer.

Understanding the Walls

Several keys emerged from my experience in being freed from my past as "Fat Kathi." One of the keys was the reality of having the walls of self-preservation and protection in my inner life removed.

A picture of Jesus and His church emerges from the Song of Solomon 2:8-9 using an example of the bride and the bridegroom. The heart of the Lord is speaking through these verses:

> *Listen! My beloved! Behold, he is coming, climbing on the mountains, leaping on the hills!*
> *My beloved is like a gazelle or a young stag. Behold, he is standing behind our wall, he is looking through the windows, he is peering through the lattice.*

Jesus is the bridegroom in this story, and He wants to come in. Yet, He is prevented by *our* wall.

A wall is anything in your life that stands between you and God. We all have walls that stop the flow of the Spirit of God and hinder intimacy with the Lord, and with other people.

Some walls are built quickly while others

70

occur over time as we add layer after layer. Without these barriers being removed, none of us can truly achieve all that God has placed us here to do.

Many of us have walls that have become our friends. We literally have a relationship with the walls and hide there any time we feel threatened. The walls protect the trauma hiding behind them. This makes us feel as though we are safe.

For those who fear letting go of any wall, we must ask the Lord, "Is it safe to let the wall go?" Then ask Him to bring you a sense of safety and well-being.

That's vitally important for people who have made friends with their walls. In my own life, I had to know it was safe to let go of the wall of fear.

Vows & Oaths

Walls can also be kept in place or sustained through inner vows or spoken oaths that we often make in moments of great pressure and strain from a traumatic event.

Jesus cautions us against making any vow or oath in Matthew 5:33-34,

> *"Again, you have heard that the ancients were told, 'You shall not make false vows, but shall fulfill your vows to the Lord.' But I say to you, make no oath at all, either by heaven, for it is the throne of God."*

The Lord's conclusion about making vows or oaths is simple. *"But let your statement be, 'yes, yes' or 'No, no'; anything beyond these is of evil,"* (verse 37). The word "evil" here in the Greek language implies an active opposition to the good. Thus, a vow or an oath can push us into a place of actually opposing good in our own lives.

Some time ago I ministered to a woman who had an incredible wall of anger in her life. As I prayed with her, she remembered as a child making a vow that people would never hurt her again.

"I won't be treated like that—ever," she vowed, and she would literally use any defense mechanism to protect herself.

After that childhood vow was renounced and her anger released, the inner turmoil and pain from her heart was set free. She was then able to integrate the parts of her heart holding onto all these things. A wonderful healing followed.

But this woman's entire healing centered upon renouncing a misspoken vow. We must guard against these vows and oaths that potentially deny us God's healing virtue in our lives.

Mad at God

Recently, I prayed for a woman in Texas who had been suffering from a debilitating fatigue for several years.

At one time, she had been given a word of knowledge that her bone marrow wasn't producing enough cells to keep her healthy because of hurt and pain in her life.

She said later she had no idea that she was mad at God. "But while we were talking, it hit me that *this* was a huge wall that I had," she wrote me later. "I realized that I had blamed God for things others had done to me."

While she was being prayed over, she later explained, "It was like poison draining out of my system." That night the presence of the Lord engulfed her and she literally laughed herself to sleep.

She later experienced flashbacks of things that had occurred at least seven or eight years earlier. "All I could do was get on my face and cry out to God for healing and closure to those episodes," she said. "I wanted those books closed and put away so I could move on."

A month later she reports: I feel safe in saying that I am healed of whatever was causing my chronic fatigue. My depression and my neck pain are gone. I keep noticing all kinds of little (and big) things that aren't wrong with me anymore...I feel like a different person."

Believing A Lie

There is little question that each of us—like the woman in the previous healing testimony—believe lies about certain incidents that occurred in our past. In her case, she blamed God for what others had done.

For instance, when molestation occurs, a child can actually believe that somehow the event was their fault. The child might feel dirty or ashamed the molestation happened.

At the death of a parent, a child can actually feel they are somehow responsible for that family member's demise. Years of struggle and difficulty can follow a child laboring under the yoke of that kind of heinous lie.

For a long time, I could not figure out why I couldn't stand the thought of seeing any kind of violence or torture on television or in movies. There were times I was physically ill and spent time in the restroom over some prison scene.

I asked the Lord to take me back to the source of this extreme behavior. I needed to know where all of these emotions were coming from.

He took me back to the attic bedroom of my family home when I was ten years of age. I shared the cute bedroom built by my dad with my sister, Karen.

All of a sudden I was back in a memory and my dad was beating Karen with a belt. She was screaming, "Stop, stop...please stop." My ears were filled with her pleading and crying.

I was terribly shaken as I witnessed this memory. I asked the Lord, "What is this about?"

"You told on her," He said, "and that's why she received that beating."

I felt the trauma of the moment. I had caused Karen to receive that beating.

"This wasn't your fault," the Lord whispered to me. "You never intended for your dad to whip her like that. It was his anger that was the problem."

A great sense of relief and healing came as the Lord ministered to me. I had believed a lie in my subconscious that I was responsible for what happened to Karen. Now I had been set free.

David understood the need for that kind of inner freedom when he wrote Psalm 51:6, *"Behold, You desire truth in the innermost being, and in the hidden part You will make me know wisdom."*

God wants us to experience His truth in our "innermost being" because many of us believe lies in the "inner parts". Our hearts will always overrule what we think to be true with our heads. The head is really no match for the heart in such circumstances.

A 'Fat' Lie

I had kept thin for many years because of a strong drive, but that all began to change when Gary and I stepped from the pastorate of a local church into a worldwide traveling ministry.

However, a combination of endless airplane travel, fatigue, sleep deprivation, and being in cultures where I couldn't eat low fat began to challenge my waist line. I also was getting older.

The result was a weight gain.

I began to feel a sense of hopelessness again as If I wasn't worth anything. These were all emotions from my past. That led me to contact a friend who had prayed with me about a lot of personal issues.

As we prayed together, the Lord pinpointed an amazing fact. When I was "Fat Kathi," I had formed an evaluation of myself that fat people weren't worth as much as thin people. It was a lie.

Thus, when I got heavier, I began to struggle with my self-worth. The Lord had to address this lie: my worth was not based on my size. It was founded upon His work of grace in me.

A lot of healing has occurred since that time. I now look at my weight as a health issue. Am I in a healthy state or not?

But I have learned—and I'm still learning—not to labor underneath the accusation of a lie. Bondage always results from believing a lie, while freedom and liberty come from embracing the truth.

The words of Jesus are well worth recalling, *"and you will know the truth, and the truth will set you free,"* (John 8:32).

Chapter 5

Liberty for the Captives

"...The Lord binds up the bruise of His people and heals the stroke of their wound."

—Isaiah 30:26 (NKJV)

I was conceived out of wedlock.

Can you imagine this scene in a small town in Ohio in 1949? My mom was an only child who had been protected all of her life and she came up pregnant. She was the high school beauty queen and my dad was the top "jock" athlete. They had plans for marriage, but I came along early.

This happened in a small town where it seemed everybody knew everything about you— including the color of your underwear that hung on the clothesline. It was the 1940s.

For years I struggled with feelings of inadequacy. No matter what I did, I always heard a voice saying, "It's not good enough." Yet, I had no understanding of where that condemning voice came from.

OPEN MY HEART, LORD

Although I had experienced freedom in some areas of my life, something was still not right. Then, I decided to go on a three-day fast.

On the third day of that fast I was standing in front of my bathroom mirror, when my life seemed to pass right before me.

I saw that all of my working with people and helping my pastor/husband were motivated by one central reason. <u>I needed to prove that I had a right to exist.</u>

I saw every place where this illegitimacy had an effect on how I handled situations. I had to make sure that everybody loved me. I had to make sure I was the perfect pastor's wife, the perfect mother, the perfect housekeeper.

Everything had to be perfect in my world because I needed validation. I seemingly went from area to area making things perfect. I always had to go overboard with everything I did.

As I stood looking at my life, the Lord began to show me that I needed validation because I felt the illegitimacy. It was still registering in my spirit.

I called a friend who had a significant ministry as an intercessor. She told me I was dealing with a spirit of illegitimacy. "This spirit is rampant in the Body of Christ," she explained.

I came to understand this spirit can manifest in a number of ways. It can come about with parents not wanting their newborn because you were a girl and they wanted a boy or vice versa.

It can come about through the great inconvenience of an unplanned pregnancy. Your spirit can feel your parents wringing their hands because you were conceived. Perhaps an older sibling died before you were born and yet, you always felt you were out of place.

When those authority figures didn't embrace you, your spirit felt that rejection. You felt you didn't have a right to be here.

Writ of Adoption

As the Lord began to give me greater understanding of the battle (and the victory to be gained) before me, I realized satan is the *supreme* legalist. He attacked Job—the most righteous man of his day—with *legal* arguments.

God had placed a hedge of protection around Job and blessed all that his hands had touched. But what would happen if it appeared God had abandoned him?

Satan predicted Job would curse God to His face. Job's answer was to plead his case before God the Father, the Judge of all the living. The story of Job's trials and ultimate triumph—often considered by scholars one of the oldest books of the Bible— contains some of the most revealing truths about good and evil.

One day as I considered my own situation (and thought of Job's trials) I came to a new-found revelation and I had an unfolding vision of a heavenly encounter involving my illegitimacy.

Suddenly, I found myself in a courtroom scene in heaven. God the Father, the Judge of all mankind, was behind the bench. Satan was marching up and down (much as he did with Job), bringing a railing accusation against me because he is the accuser of the brethren.

"I have a right to torment her with fear leading to slavery," the devil said pointing at me. "She was not wanted by her parents. She was conceived out of wedlock and doesn't have a right to be here.

The basic fact was inescapable: I was uncovered and illegitimate. It meant I didn't have a right to be there *legally* in the courts of heaven.

As satan continued berating me, Jesus suddenly rushed into the courtroom through a massive set of doors. I noticed He had a piece of paper in His hand.

"Father, I have a Writ of Adoption for this one," He announced, "and it's signed in My blood."

And with that declaration, Jesus picked me up and took me behind the bench actually placing me in the lap of the Father. What a scene!

The Writ of Adoption actually comes into place when a landowner's son or daughter reaches a certain age and has the full legal rights of an heir. Prior to that age, they were treated no better than a slave.

Those are the same legal rights as the Lord Jesus has!

By His adoption (written and sealed in His precious blood), each of us becomes a total heir with Him, actually sitting in the lap of the Father.

That is not the same as an orphan adoption. This is the coming of age of a *true* son and being placed in the lap of the Father to be mentored and disciplined by Him. In this special place, we will *"be subject to the Father of spirits and live"* (Hebrews 12:9) and *"share His holiness"* (Hebrews 12:10).

It became a liberating day in my life when I discovered my adoption as a legal heir with the Lord Jesus. My life has not been the same. The Bible speaks about this adoption in the following Scriptures. Please examine them with me.

> For you have not received a spirit of slavery leading to fear again, but you have received **a spirit of adoption** as sons by which we cry out, "Abba! Father!" (Romans 8:15).

> And not only this, but also we ourselves having the first fruits of the Spirit, even we ourselves groan within ourselves, waiting eagerly for our **adoption as sons**, the redemption of our body. (Romans 8:23).

> ...who are Israelites, to whom belongs the **adoption as sons** and the glory and the covenants and the giving of the Law

and the temple service and the promises. (Romans 9:4).

...in order that He might redeem those who were under the Law, that we might receive the **adoptions as sons**.
And because you are sons, God has sent forth the Spirit of His Son into our hearts, crying, "Abba! Father!" (Galatians 4:5-6).

He predestined us to **adoption as sons** through Jesus Christ to Himself, according to the kind intentions of His will. (Ephesians 1:5).

Our Adoption

The adoption spoken of in these Scriptures meant something similar to the Hebrew and Greek mind of that day—a son or daughter coming of age.

Perhaps that basic revelatory understanding has changed somewhat in our day. We believe the Father puts His Spirit (His DNA, if you will) in us at the new birth, making us a new creation.

When the Lord Jesus presented you as an adopted son or daughter, it means "as a full son or daughter." In the Hebrew, it means "having the full rights of inheritance."

As an adopted child of God, that person would not longer be treated as a servant, but as a genuine son, given to the Father to be mentored at His side.

The Lord Jesus has placed each of us in the Father's hands for mentoring. That's what Hebrews 12:7 tells us: *"If you endure chastening, God deals with you as with sons; for what son is there whom a father does not chasten?"*

Many of God's children experience this unpleasant chastening. We interpret it to mean something evil has come against us. But, God is allowing us to be placed in circumstances where we have to face things about ourselves.

Hopefully, the result will be that we stop working out of the pain of our past and start living in the freedom and liberty of our blessed relationship with the Holy Spirit.

Jesus on the Cross

Another liberating key that I discovered along the way was the reality of what the Lord Jesus Christ did on the Cross for every man and woman on the face of the earth. They no longer have to carry the pain of their past.

The Amplified Bible conveys this great truth in 2 Corinthians 5:21:

> *For our sake He made Christ [virtually] to be sin Who knew no sin, so that in and through Him we might become [endued with, viewed as being in, and examples of] the righteousness of God [what we ought to be, approved and acceptable and in right relationship with Him, by His goodness].*

The Message Bible says simply: *"God put the wrong on Him who never did anything wrong, so we could be put right with God."*

The Lord's sacrifice of Himself on the Cross stands as a magnet for our lives. His sacrifice pulled all of the pain, the anger, the shame, fear, terror, and rejection upon Himself. The Son of God died so that we could *experientially* be freed from those negative emotions.

God's purpose in the Cross is also expressed in Romans 15:3, and connects with David's writing in Psalm 69:9. *"For even Christ did not please Himself; but as it is written, 'The reproaches of those who reproached You fell on Me'."*

At the Cross, the reproaches of those people— who had dishonored and reproached God, and were mad at Him because of their lives—even fell upon Jesus. He took those reproaches on the Cross so we wouldn't have to anymore. He took all of our anger against God on the Cross, all of our dishonoring of God, all of our misconceptions about God. It was all nailed to His Cross.

The best known prophecy of the Crucifixion in the Bible is found in Isaiah 53, which is later quoted by both Matthew and Peter. Not only does Isaiah give us an accurate picture of the Crucifixion, he also speaks of the purpose of the Cross.

In verse four, he writes: *"Surely our griefs He Himself bore, and our sorrows He carried; yet we ourselves esteemed Him stricken, smitten of God, and afflicted."*

So, the suffering of the Cross clearly enables me to be forgiven of sin, to find peace in this life, and healing for my body.

The Amplified Bible gives us further understanding about verse four. *"Surely He has borne our griefs (sicknesses, weaknesses, and distresses) and carried our sorrows and pains..."*

In some of the workshops, I ask the Lord to make real to the audience what Jesus did on the Cross. They can now be freed from the grief, sorrow, and pain of the past because those toxic emotions were nailed to His cross.

Jesus is the only One who wants these emotions. He took them upon Himself so we would not have to. In reality, we do not have to carry these emotions anymore.

Shame can be added to that list of emotions. Jesus hung naked, bleeding, and dying on that Cross. He was exposed before the whole world. He was shamed perhaps more than any man on the face of the earth.

But Hebrews 12:2 (Amplified Bible) gives us a triumphant picture of what happened on the Cross. *"...He, for the joy [of obtaining the prize] that was set before Him, endured the cross, despising and ignoring the shame, and is now seated at the right hand of the throne of God."*

Jesus denied shame an avenue to function in Him as He submitted to the will of God. Now, none of us ever have to yield to the shame of our past.

Whatever you have stuffed down into your insides is a defeated foe because of our victorious Savior.

The reality is that we don't have to carry these burdens anymore. Whatever name they are called—guilt, shame, sadness, sorrow, pain—were all nailed to the Cross of Jesus Christ.

That's what *true* freedom is.

A Vision of the Cross

The young woman (I mentioned earlier in Chapter 3), who was released from a traumatic childhood of sexual abuse, had a magnificent vision one day of her life intertwining with Jesus on the Cross.

"I found myself, still as a young girl, wrapped around Him as He hung on the Cross," she explained of the vision.

"I wept for Him as He anguished, and yet as He anguished He comforted me, and I could feel my pain leaving me and flowing into Him.

"With one look into my eyes, He made me to know that all was well. I rested with my arms tightly looped around his neck as He died, and my pain and my sin of rejecting Him had its death in Him."

Her life was profoundly changed. "The Lord made this little girl understand that there is great evil in this world," she told me. "But His death on the Cross is my justice and vindication, and His resurrection is my healing and transformation."

Chapter 6

The Church: A Healing Community

"For you have been unfaithful with that which I entrusted to you. For I waited for mercy and compassion and understanding to arise in you. I waited for you to bind up My brokenhearted in your congregations—for you to reach out your hand of compassion to the oppressed—for you to have mercy upon those upon whom I would mete mercy. But none of these you have done."

—from *Journal of the Unknown Prophet* by Wendy Alec

Jesus' mandate to the church was not only to set the captive free, but to heal the brokenhearted. That's what Isaiah 61 is all about, *"...He has sent me to heal the brokenhearted...,"* (NKJV).

Connecting with Isaiah's prophecy, Jesus boldly claims to be the promised Messiah (Luke 4:18-19, *New Living Translation*) where He defines the message of the kingdom of God.

The Spirit of the Lord is upon me, for He has appointed me to preach Good

News to the poor. He has sent me to proclaim that captives will be released, that the blind will see, that the downtrodden will be freed from their oppressors, and that the time of the Lord's favor has come.

The Amplified Bible enlarges the scope of our understanding by identifying the oppressed the Messiah will set free, in verse 18, as those *"downtrodden, bruised, crushed, and broken down by calamity."*

Luke makes it clear that Jesus passed this same ministry on to the disciples (Luke 9:1-2), and ultimately to the entire New Testament church (Acts 1:1-2).

The church has cast out demons for a long time. There have been whole ministries centered on casting out demons but very few have come on the scene focused upon healing the brokenhearted.

Demons are like flies around garbage. When traumatic events occur or when we sin on a continual basis, these demons attach themselves to those areas of impurity and imperfection.

But deliverance is only one part of what Jesus Christ came to earth to provide for mankind.

A Personal Testimony

When Gary and I were first married, my experience with the Baptism of the Holy Spirit seemed to bring forth a demonic encounter in my life. I had an obsessive fear and could not seem to get away from it no matter what I did.

I knew that it was a spirit of witchcraft handed down from my grandmother who had been a spiritist. I had not been involved in spiritism but it came down through the generations. I had been an open, uncovered vessel.

As is always the case in satan's kingdom, the basis for that attachment is fear. I was afraid to let this *thing* go because it had become so much a part of me. It was illogical but still overwhelming.

One long night of wrestling with this demonic force, I had a vision of this round orb-like light in the middle of my body. Jesus was in the center and there were myriads of people and angels too.

I recognized the Lord had literally placed the kingdom of God inside of me. I realized I was afraid to let this demon go because I didn't feel safe. When I turned and cried out to Jesus, "help me let this go," the thing *instantly* left. I never had that fear again.

Deliverance is a valid ministry of setting the captive free. But, my single experience of being freed from fear did not include freeing me from anger or control, which were demonic strongholds in my life. These struggles were rooted in wounds, hurts, and rejection.

Once I started having my broken heart healed, though, it was simultaneous that any demonic force feeding on those things also left. The deliverance came and freedom remained.

OPEN MY HEART, LORD

God's Call for the Church

The history of the church is strewn with the corpses of fallen men (and women) of God who began with great gifts and world-wide ministries developed around themselves. Unquestionably, these were people of talent and ability who were genuinely called and anointed of the Holy Spirit.

Yet, underneath the smiles and happy faces were traumas and pains from their early lives that had never been healed. Somehow these patterns of the heart were never connected to Jesus and healed.

In time the pressures of the ministry exposed the hidden pains of the heart. Personal destruction often resulted. Ministries folded. The world had a hearty laugh from the pain of God's ministers.

Yet, God never intended for the pressures of life—or the struggles of our inner life—to drive us from the ministry. If we are healed from our brokenness, we can be sustained in our calling.

Wendy Alec's classic book, *Journal of the Unknown Prophet* speaks prophetically to these issues of unhealed traumas and emotional injuries which have become invitations for demonic attack:

"Many, many of My children did not receive healing of their minds, emotions and souls in this last generation. And because they have lived in the household of God for years, many do not even realize that these scarred places exist.

"These last days' assignments have been meticulously strategized, and that is the very

90

strength of their evil—they have been tailor-made to each of My champions. They know the urgent, driving, unmet needs of the soul; the generational bondages of each individual called by Me to impact this generation; the lack of nurturing; the deep unhealed rejections and hurts of the emotions; the fatherlessness; the need for affirmation; the desire to belong; the deep isolations—all of which when not met in Me—now have laid the perfect snare for the assignments of the enemy."

The time has come for the church to get all that kind of living cleaned up. God is showing us how the spiritual realm operates. He's revealing how to get cleaned up, how to be made whole and to know the reality of our salvation.

In Psalm 51 David speaks about knowing our salvation and understanding what God has done for us. He prays for God to *"create in me a clean heart, and then I will teach transgressors their way."*

The world has laughed at Christians and the church. They see the church in as much of a mess as they are—or even worse. At least, they admit where they're at. We tend to cover it up with a lot of religious talk.

Ultimately, the church (and God's people) must come to the place of understanding this pain and unrest in our hearts. What is this trouble on my insides? Why are my thoughts and habits seemingly so far from God?

The writer of Proverbs 16:2 looks beyond the mere eyesight to issues of the heart saying, *"All the ways of a man are clean in his own sight, but the Lord weighs the motives."*

The Amplified Bible provides us with an even broader understanding of that same verse. *"All the ways of a man are pure in his own eyes, but the Lord weighs the spirits (the thoughts and intents of the heart)."*

I believe the time has come for God's church to come to grips with what is motivating us. Is it religion? Selfish ambition? Or, is there something more sinister and evil controlling my life?

As a leader, I have inadvertently and stupidly hurt others because of things that were wrong with me. It took me a long time to understand how my woundedness affected my dealings with others.

It is time for God's church to stand up and ask forgiveness for the hurts we've caused and for those who have been attempting to build their own kingdoms. It has always been wrong and it is now time for those kingdoms to topple.

There is only one King. His name is Jesus Christ. May His kingdom come; may His will be done here on earth, as it is in heaven.

God has called His church to be an honest, transparent, and healing community. We obviously can't move into that arena until we're cleaned up. It's really about getting our broken hearts healed so we're not laboring out of pain any more.

Once again, *Journal of the Unknown Prophet*

confronts this issue:

"Some of My champions have experienced a violent, satanic assailing against their minds. Any thought not taken captive shall be a thought that can take violent root in their souls to lead to ensnarement. Anything from their past that has been dealt with by their own strength and not by My Spirit shall become a snare to them and can leave them vulnerable to the enemy of their souls. Any habit not ruthlessly dealt with and put to the cross...will breed and rapidly multiply."

Questions & Answers

Often I am asked questions about some points of my teaching, and I'd like to answer a few of those at this point.

What about the issue of forgiveness in receiving healing? Isn't this the key to most healing?

Many people I have spoken with on this subject say they have been told to forgive someone "as an act of their will" or to keep "re-forgiving" until they get results.

Much of this type of forgiveness is noble but is in our heads. Neither does it go to the full extent of what Jesus wants. He was very clear on this subject. *"My heavenly Father will also do the same to you, if each of you does not forgive his brother from your heart,"* (Matthew 18:35, emphasis added).

Jesus says people who don't forgive from the

heart will be handed over to the torturers (verse 34)!

The kind of forgiveness Jesus is talking about is the complete loosing in every dimension and from every emotion towards the offending person so that the forgiving person is no longer connected in any manner. This frees us to love those who have persecuted and harmed us.

I believe it is difficult to honestly forgive when we are still in great pain. I am of the opinion that when we have our hearts healed and cleansed from the pain, genuine forgiveness will come easily.

Then, we will be able to release the offending person. Perhaps we will even gain a deeper understanding of why that person did what they did.

What about repentance? Is there a role for biblical repentance in healing of the brokenhearted?

I believe this is a way of repentance because you are facing what is inside of your heart. The Lord is coming by His Spirit and reprogramming the way you think.

In a certain sense, repentance means to change the way one thinks. This process is all about allowing the Lord to come into our hearts and change the way we think about what has happened in our lives.

The apostle Paul described challenges us in this manner: "*And be constantly renewed in the spirit of your mind [having a fresh mental and spiritual attitude],"* (Ephesians 4:23, Amplified).

This is not some kind of mental gymnastics, but a renewing of the inner core of your life. It means to lay aside the patterns of thinking from your old life, along with the garbage of the past.

The Message Bible portrays Ephesians 4:23 in this way: *"And then take on an entirely new way of life—a God-fashioned life, a life renewed from the inside as God accurately reproduces His character in you."*

I believe this process will ultimately change your behavior and bring healing and repentance to your liberated heart.

How is this process of healing related to putting away "childish things" according to 1 Corinthians 13:11?

Paul says in this verse, *"When I was a child, I used to speak like a child, think like a child, reason like a child; when I became a man, I did away with childish things."*

This healing process is a way of putting away childish things. When you allow the Lord to come in and take the pain of whatever that child was holding, healing will come. You will be able to receive that disconnected child or part back into your adult heart.

Chapter 7

A Time of Prayer

"Train me, God, to walk straight; then I'll follow Your true path. Put me together, one heart and mind; then, undivided, I'll worship in joyful fear."

—*Psalm 86:11-12, from The Message Bible*

I have prayed prayers similar to this with thousands of people in a variety of settings on several continents. The prayer is made all together—most of the time—without personally laying hands on anyone.

As I pray this prayer, I want you to expect a touch from Almighty God. Expect Him to manifest His presence in your life. Receive this prayer and pause several times to savor the Lord's presence with you.

We are going to ask the Holy Spirit to come into our midst...we are just asking the Lord to bring up in you whatever He wants to heal.

Some of you will see things...some of you will feel things...some of you will hear things...some of you will sense things. Some of you will have impressions. There is no right or wrong way...we are just here to receive from the Lord.

Holy Spirit, we thank You for coming today. We thank You for Your heart to be manifested to us today. Lord, we honor You, that You heal the brokenhearted.

We ask that You come now. Lord, I specifically ask that You send Your angels of healing to this room...send Your troops, Your healing troops. I pray that they are stationed in this room and that every person's angel is activated to assist in the healing process.

For those who are sincerely believing for healing, I want you to ask the Lord, "What does He want to bring up in my life? What do You want to heal in me?"

We just wait upon Him. Relax. Take a deep breath. Let the Lord do it in you.

Walls

If you are seeing blackness, that is a wall. Ask the Lord, "What is that wall? Why are You bringing this up?" Whatever is coming to you, ask "why?"

If you see a wall, ask the Lord to come and minister to this wall. "Lord, will you come and heal this wall in my life?"

Some of you had a situation come up. A

memory. A thought. Ask the Lord, "Why did You bring that up? What do You want to heal?"

Anger

Some of you may feel as if you are not getting anywhere with the Lord. That usually is an indication of anger because it blocks hearing from the Lord.

If you are not able to feel or sense the Lord's presence, anger could be stopping you. Some of you have controlled others with anger. Are you willing to let the Lord take the anger and replace it with Himself?

God is the only One who wants your anger. Ask Him to take all the anger out of your heart. Release it to Him.

Ask the Lord to help you get in touch with that anger and then ask Him to come and lift this anger from you. "Right now...just pull it out of me and into You, Lord Jesus."

Remember the reproaches of those who opposed God all fell upon Jesus at the cross. He took all the anger upon Himself at the cross. Right now, allow Him to pull it out of you and into the cross.

Just keep asking until you feel a real release of the anger...until you feel that anger lifting out of you and into Him. Some of you may feel this anger has been such a friend. Ask the Lord: "Is it safe to let this anger go?" Now listen carefully to what He says and follow His directions.

Pain

Some of you may have tapped into some pain in your life. "Come and take this pain out of me and into You, Lord. I just give You all the pain." Some of you may begin to feel heavy or weep; you may want to cry. Go ahead and allow that to happen and then release it to God.

You no longer need to live with this pain. You've felt it before...now you can just release it into Him and ask Him to quickly pull out the pain. Ask Him "Is it safe to feel the pain?" Then, release it into Him.

Shame

If shame of any kind is coming up, ask the Lord to begin to pull the shame out of you and into Him. Ask the Lord if He would release you from any guilt and take that guilt and shame from you and into Him.

Lord, I ask in the Name of Jesus that You release anyone bound by shame. I ask that You release anyone who is guilt-driven. Some of you have been made to feel ashamed you are the way you are. Just allow the Holy Spirit to remove this guilt and shame and pull it from you and into Him.

Molestation

Some of you have been made to feel ashamed because you have been molested. Your shame was tied to the molestation. Ask the Lord how did He see the situation that shamed your life. Listen to His voice and release this shame into Him.

For those of you who have been molested, under any circumstances, I now release you from the spirit of the person who did that to you. Lord, I defeat the shame within these people in the Name of Jesus.

I come against and pull out of these people any spirit of any person who overtook their little spirits. The residue of the molester that was left behind is pulled out in the Name of Jesus. I release you from any spirit of control, witchcraft and manipulation that was over you.

In the Name of Jesus, I release negative words spoken over these people and especially the words spoken over themselves from the pain they endured. I release death from their spirit connected to them being molested.

Word Curses

The Lord has shown me that the spirit of life and death is in the tongue. Words carry spiritual substance either for life or death.

Lord, I ask You to release people from the death that has been given in their spirits by word curses spoken over them.

I especially come against words that were demeaning, degrading and abusive spoken by people in authority. I pull the death spirit out of those words and I release it from any destructive force in any believer's life.

Bitterness

I pull out any roots of bitterness from the hearts of the people...any spirit of bitterness dwelling within you. Some of you will feel something just lift off your shoulders. Others will sense it come right out of your heart. A few of you will possibly feel a heat in your body.

Illegitimacy

This prayer is for those who feel they have never had a right to be here. You feel you were never wanted. I come against a spirit of illegitimacy that has attached itself to the people of God.

I command you in the Name of Jesus to release your hold on anyone's life. You are not longer allowed to work that spirit against any child of God. You will now go in the Name of Jesus.

Little Person/Part

Now listen carefully.

Some of you will become aware of a little person or a part of your heart. You may see that person or part. How is that little person or part feeling? Are they feeling pain, shame or fear? What was the trauma? Is that little person or part feeling very alone?

Ask the Lord to come and minister to that

little person or part right now. Watch and see what He does. That little person or part held the junk of your life for such a long time.

Are you ready to embrace that little person or part who held all that pain and guilt? Ask the Lord to help you in this process. Tell that person or part: I'm so sorry I left you behind with all that pain. Come and be a part of me again. I promise not to leave you behind.

For some of you, it may seem like two pieces of a puzzle coming together. For some of you, it may appear like the blending of two people. God will do it differently with each person; simply let the process happen. Don't try to force it.

If you feel uncomfortable at this point, you're not ready. There is a good chance some pain or residue of pain remains in your heart. If you can't take this step right now, leave that little person or part with the Lord. You can do this later.

Some of you may have more than one part inside of you. There may be different ages of trauma in your life. (You can utilize this process over and over in prayer as the Lord brings up these parts of your life. Then—with His help—release the pain and trauma, and allow the cycle to be repeated as the Lord directs you.)

Revelation of Adoption

Lord, I pray for a spirit of revelation of adoption to be released now that each one would receive their adoption and what it means in their innermost being. They have been bought by the blood of Jesus Christ. Release in them what it means to be a child of God with full rights of inheritance in Jesus' Name.

Revelation of the Lord

How do you see the Lord? What do you think of when you consider the living God?

Lord, please given them a revelation of Who You really are. You are the only One who can truly reveal Yourself to mankind...Your Bible is filled with examples of how this has been done for thousands of years.

I ask that You grant Your people a revelation of our Savior—the Lord Jesus Christ. I ask for a revelation of the blessed Holy Spirit. I ask for a revelation of the Father. Thank You for this magnificent Trinity—the Three in One!

EPILOGUE

Somehow this dimension of inner healing opens the door to the supernatural realm with God.

That is clearly my own personal experience—and thousands of others as well—people who have received healing for their broken hearts typically step into a new arena of the supernatural with the Lord.

It has happened to ordinary people—and church leaders alike—from South America to Norway to Canada to cities all across America.

Your question is a simple one: Where do I go from here?

You've read the book, now listen to the CD and receive the ministry of the Holy Spirit in the healing of your broken heart. Be prepared for some awesome events to happen in your life.

If you need the help of a competent Christian counselor or therapist, please see our website, *www.GaryOates.com* for a list of someone potentially in your area.

APPENDIX A

HEALING
THE BROKENHEARTED

This appendix is a collaborative effort of Andrew A. Miller, MSW, LCSW, and Scott Flanagan, Ph.D. The material presented here is material that we have presented in our teaching as faculty at Tallahassee's Center for Biblical Studies, in conjunction with Tallahassee Healing Prayer Ministries.

Nothing in this material guarantees any result or outcome. It should also be understood that the use of the principles outlined in this appendix in the context of inner healing ministry is not a substitute for therapy. Persons who display dissociative symptoms are encouraged to seek counseling with Christian mental health professionals trained in the fields of dissociation and trauma.

Andy has had an extensive professional background working with dissociation and has developed a unique set of tools for dealing with this form of emotional wounding. Therefore, in the section that outlines the steps in healing the brokenhearted, he will revert to the first person narration to identify the clinical experience he draws on to explain the procedures.

When we were asked to write an appendix for Kathi's book, we were excited because the ministry to the brokenhearted has been so central to our own healings. It has also constituted Andy's calling, both in ministry and professional practice. We have come to regard this ministry as being essential to Christ's own mission statement established at the onset of His ministry. The gospel of Luke records the amazing announcement of this mission (*King James Version*):

And when He (Jesus) had opened the book (Isaiah), He found the place where it is written, the Spirit of the Lord is upon Me, because He hath anointed Me to preach the gospel to the poor; He hath sent Me to heal the brokenhearted, to preach deliverance to the captive, and recovering of sight to the blind, to set at liberty them that are bruised, to preach the acceptable year of the Lord.

Luke 4:17-19

In His last days before the crucifixion, Jesus makes it clear that He would make provision for this ministry to continue through the agent of the Holy Spirit and His disciples (*New International Version*):

I tell you the truth, anyone who has faith in Me will do what I have been doing. He will do even greater things than these, because I am going to the Father...

If you love Me, you will obey what I command. And I will ask the Father, and He will give you another Counselor to be with you forever—the Spirit of truth...But the Counselor, the Holy Spirit, whom the Father will send in My name, will teach you all things and will remind you of everything I have said to you.

John 14:12, 15-17, 26

I have much more to say to you, more than you can now bear. But when He, the Spirit of truth comes, He will guide you into all truth...He will bring glory to Me by taking from what is Mine and making it known to you.

John 16:12-14

To the Jews who had believed Him, Jesus said, "If you hold to my teaching, you are really My disciples. Then you will know the truth, and the truth will set you free."

John 8:31-32

While our contribution is mainly in the area of emotional healing (healing the brokenhearted), it is interesting that physical healing (i.e., restoring sight to the blind) was never intended to be excluded from healing the brokenhearted. It also would be accurate to say that healing the brokenhearted was never intended to be excluded from physical healing ministry. And yet, that is just what we see today. So it is exciting for us to see both forms of healing prominently displayed in Gary's and Kathi's ministry.

This central mission of Christ—to heal the brokenhearted and to bring release to the captives—is largely ignored or given back seat in the present day mission of the church. There have been many authors who have written about inner healing. And there are perhaps thousands of small, church-based healing ministries, and yet they are mostly cast as minor programs, supportive to more teaching oriented ministries.

Teaching is an important ministry, but when it is elevated above binding up the brokenhearted, it often fails to seriously impact those who are stuck in painful captivity. It is for the hope of seeing these captives set free that we join Kathi Oates in co-laboring in this central mission of "healing the brokenhearted."

While Scott already had a prior relationship with Gary and Kathi, our healing-oriented relationship began several years ago when we were invited to facilitate basic classes in Theophostic Prayer Ministry at Gary's and Kathi's church. They had determined that God was calling them to establish a healing ministry. What caught our attention was that they understood that they needed the same level of healing as the folks to which they were ministering. In our experience, it is unusual for church leaders to acknowledge that they need this level of healing.

Since the prayer ministers in the Oates' church were mostly novices, Kathi and Gary would ask for ministry meetings with us. Kathi received ministry similar to the experiences described in this book and immediately began to apply the truth of those experiences in sessions that she was facilitating. Then she assisted Andy in ministering to an advanced case of Dissociative Identity Disorder. As we moved forward, it began to become apparent that these principles not only applied to severe forms of dissociation, but to all of us.

What eventually emerged out of all this was a kind of healing community where any one of us had absolute freedom to approach another twosome to address a place of brokenness that needed healing. Aside from the importance of the principals contained in this book, we are coming to believe that participation in the next wave of God in His church will require the establishment of communities that freely participate in healing the brokenhearted—laymen and leaders alike.

When Gary was caught up into heaven, within a short period of time, it became clear that God was releasing the Oates from pastoral ministry and raising up another form of ministry–the ministry of healing evangelists. First came the reports of creative physical miracles. But what surprised us all was when Gary and Kathi came home from a trip and reported the results of Kathi ministering the inner healing principles contained in this book in mass settings.

The healing fruit she was witnessing and the many reports of emotional healing marked the opening of a major new phase in the development of inner healing ministries. The mass healings in large settings that she is seeing reveal the heart of God to see His church set free. This is part of the end times acceleration of the work of the Holy Spirit.

We have worked hard to present the principles that under gird Kathi's ministry in a concise manner. While Andy's clinical observations have helped to solidify these principles, and there is much research which can support these observations, our conviction fell along the line of not overwhelming the reader with clinical research that requires a graduate degree to understand. There are, however, several references, and we have borrowed freely from the excellent work of several pioneers in this field. We have also provided an understandable glossary of terms used in this book.

A general weakness of Christian literature is the conspicuous absence of biblical language to describe the features of dissociation. It's not an issue of using biblical language in order to justify this ministry. Rather, research and clinical observations simply support biblical truth that has been there all through the ages. This has always been God's ministry which He entrusted to the church. In generations past, the church has abdicated its responsibility to participate in this ministry, but it seems clear that once again, God is giving it back to the church, most especially to the layman.

It is our sincere hope that these principles are easily understood. We have begun with a brief description of inner healing, followed by a section on the origins of our emotional problems, with its accompanying beliefs and defense mechanisms.

Following this, we develop the concepts of the wounded child and alter personalities, and show how the DID model serves to sharpen our awareness of what is occurring in all levels of brokenness. With these similarities understood, we identify three kinds of brokenheartedness on the continuum of dissociation. With this, we're then ready to present the healing process, which includes the brokenhearted model, a reconciliation script and discussion regarding the need to release trauma, followed by the need for Spirit infilling.

What Is Inner Healing?

Inner healing is the healing of our emotional wounds, wounds that we initially experienced in our early childhood. These woundings and experiences often become repressed with time, and thus remain hidden and festering within us, poisoning our souls and distorting our beliefs and behavior. As a result, we become chained to and locked into dysfunctional patterns of thinking, relating, and acting, patterns such as fear, anxiety, anger, conflict, confusion, guilt, shame, remorse, and depression.

We all need inner healing because we have all been wounded emotionally to some degree or another. We all tend to suppress emotional wounds, but that doesn't make them go away. Rather, they fester and tend to cause us increasing and re-occurring problems as adults.

Inner healing is available for all of us and we believe that it is part of the work that the Lord wants to do in us. As David says in Psalm 51, *"You desire truth in the inner parts,"* because the lies hidden in our belief systems and the defense mechanisms that we have erected to cope with the pain associated with our lies hurt us and those around us. More importantly, they create obstacles for our coming into a more intimate relationship with God.

The Origins of our Emotional Problems

To understand how to heal emotional issues, it is helpful to understand how these problems develop in the first place. Mary Pitches (1987, 1990, 1996) presents us with a model of the origins of our emotional woundings. When children are growing up, they need the three S's – security, self-worth and significance – security (the feeling of protection, that their needs are being taken care of), self-worth (the sense that they are valued, and special and loved unconditionally for just who they are) and significance (that what they do is important and meaningful, that they are recognized as capable and that their contributions are appreciated).

The problem is that most of us come from dysfunctional families because we live in a fallen world. Even if our parents were saintly, we are all likely to have experienced emotional wounding as a child without the opportunity of getting healed.

The basic issue here is that children do not know how to take their pain to God, and often do not have a parent that can help them in the healing process. So instead they try to develop coping mechanisms to avoid the pain. As children, we try to solve the problem ourselves, a problem that only God's love and truth can solve. In reality we, as children, are trying to heal ourselves and that is a sin, because only Jesus can heal us.

We cannot blame ourselves or blame children for doing this. It is all that the child knows to do. As a result, children develop protective patterns of behavior that serve as functional coping mechanisms to protect themselves from the pain. However, they carry these coping mechanisms into adult life and, as adults, these patterns become dysfunctional strongholds that distort our relationship with others; they are self-defeating and often lead to addictions and other patterns aimed at covering and stuffing the pain and emotional scars of the past.

It is useful to understand that when children are wounded, they do two things: 1) they create a belief or perception about the incident and 2) they try to come up with a coping mechanism for dealing with the problem.

Creating a Belief – Children are very egocentric in the way they view and interpret their world. When something traumatic, painful, fearful, embarrassing or shameful happens to them, they tend to believe that it is their fault. If their parents get divorced, they tend to think it was because of something they did. If their father sexually abuses them, they believe that somehow they caused it to happen. If their mother beats them, they instinctively think that it was because they did something wrong. This tendency to personalize trauma is often reinforced by verbal messages from the one inflicting the pain, telling them that it was their fault. Most likely, the child was completely innocent or just being a child, but all that matters is what the child believes. When children interpret traumatic events through their egocentric screens, they come up with explanatory beliefs, such as:

I am bad, dirty, shameful.
I am stupid, ignorant, incompetent.
I am not loved or wanted.
I am worthless. I have no value

I am all alone. No one cares.

Here we are very much indebted to Dr. Ed Smith and his principles of Theophostic Prayer Ministry (TPM). TPM teaches us that the negative emotions associated with a memory come not from what happened to us, bad as it might have been, but from the lie that we believed about ourselves as a result of the experience. The memory is not the source of the pain but the container for the pain. The pain comes from the lie, and as long as that wounded child believes in that lie, the lie will continue to stir up negative emotions.[1]

Creating a Defense Mechanism – As a child, what do you do when something bad happens to

---

[1] TPM is an integral part of our prayer ministry and we highly recommend that those wanting to get involved in inner healing ministry acquire the TPM training materials and learn and practice the principles in a small group context. In its simplest form, Theophostic Prayer Ministry can be seen as a four-step process.

1. We ask the prayer recipient to **get in touch with the feelings** associated with some recent incident in their lives that stirred up negative emotions.
2. We have the recipient focus on the painful emotions, let go of the recent event and allow Jesus to take them **back to the source and origin** of those emotions, to an earlier, typically childhood memory that matches the emotions they are feeling.
3. We ask the recipient to focus on the painful emotions associated with the early memory and **ask the "why" questions to uncover the lie** they believed.
4. We ask the recipient to stay in touch with the emotions associated with the lie the child believed and **ask Jesus to reveal His truth**. When Jesus speaks His truth into that wounded little child place, the memory does not change, but the pain associated with it disappears and is replaced with peace and calm.

you? Children are survivors. They figure out a way to protect themselves from ever having to suffer from that pain or humiliation again. Wounded children instinctively try to rescue themselves by building up their own flesh, providing for their own needs and protection, and relying on their own strength. The child's coping strategy often serves his or her immediate survival needs well, but over time, becomes increasingly problematic. Over time, the defense mechanism tends to work less well and the pain leaks through. As adults, our childhood coping strategies have become subconscious reactions and so when triggered, we tend to apply them in more exaggerated forms, resulting in self-defeating behaviors.

The Sins of Our Beliefs and Behavioral Coping Mechanisms

While the child is only doing the best he or she can to survive, our model highlights two major kinds of unconscious sins that the child is committing which must be addressed in the healing process.

1) **The Belief** – The first unconscious sin is the beliefs that the child forms in the aftermath of the childhood experience (a traumatic event or a modeled behavior or teaching). Mary Pitches (1996) simply calls these beliefs; Chester and Betsy Kylstra (1996) refer to them as ungodly beliefs and Ed Smith (2005) as lies. An ungodly belief is a belief, decision, attitude, or agreement that does not agree with God (His Word, His nature, and His character). The perfect ungodly belief is one that appears to be absolutely true based on the facts of our

experience and yet is absolutely false based on God's Word – e.g., No one loves me; I am all alone; I am defective; or God doesn't love me. Ungodly beliefs are sin because they bring us out of agreement with God and into agreement with satan.

2) **The Defense Mechanism** – The second sin associated with the child's response to an emotionally wounding event is found in his or her instinctive coping strategy. The child's unconscious solution is to try to fix the problem and protect himself (herself) from further pain without turning to God. This gets back to the child's innate sin nature – "I do it myself." Wounded children instinctively try to rescue themselves by providing for their own needs and protection, and relying on their own strength. This approach serves their immediate survival needs well, but over time, becomes an increasing problem. What the child is doing is building walls (defense mechanisms) based on a rotten foundation (lies). The beliefs (lies) and the behavior patterns (defense mechanisms, walls) become our self-made prisons that keep the healing light of Christ out of our lives. Because our solution has left God out, our healing cannot come until we are willing to tear down our walls and let God in.

In Jeremiah 2:13, the Lord says: *"My people have committed two sins: They have forsaken me, the spring of living water, and have dug their own cisterns, broken cisterns that cannot hold water."*

The first sin is that we have rejected God, broken agreement with Him and come into agreement with the lies of the devil. The second sin is that we have tried to fix ourselves by our own devices, with our own broken cisterns. These broken cisterns, or defense mechanisms are incapable of fixing anything, but we cling to them anyway.

The emphasis here on the child's defense mechanisms alerts us to the fact that more is involved in our model of the origins of emotional problems and dysfunctional behavior patterns than just beliefs. The child's defense mechanisms typically include inner vows, bitter root judgments, walls of dissociation, repression, denial, avoidance, perfectionism, etc., and wrong choices. Wrong choices are sinful behaviors that are made in an effort to self-medicate and comfort our emotional wounds. In fact, they make our problems worse and lead to addictive behaviors.

All of the above plus unforgiveness of ourselves, God, and others, are blocks to our healing. God will not remove these obstacles to our healing, when we are the ones that have constructed them. By our own choice, we have built walls to protect ourselves from pain. Since He has given us free will, He will not pull down walls that we have chosen to put up. We have stuffed down the pain inside us and sealed it off from our consciousness, but it is eating us alive. We are bound in chains in a dungeon of our own making. We have to be willing to break down the walls we have built to protect ourselves and face the pain before we can, in essence, invite Jesus in and give Him permission to heal our emotional woundedness.

Defense Mechanisms as Walls

Theophostic Prayer Ministry emphasizes the lies but only acknowledges in passing the existence of defense mechanisms as one of many forms of clutter than can impede the healing process. Recall that defense mechanisms are the child's solution to dealing with painful experiences. These are walls, which are directed outward to protect the child from having a similar painful experience in the environment in which he or she is living. These walls attempt to guard against a reoccurrence of the painful experience. But while building walls to protect ourselves from future pain from the external environment, we also seal off and hold in the pain of the original wounding experience, where it festers and occasionally leaks out.

Those of us practicing TPM have found that the walls can be a major obstacle to the healing process. The prayer recipient has held on to them so tightly for so long that they feel normal and necessary, no matter how dysfunctional they are in their lives. When we begin to approach a memory holding pain, the walls go up. That is their function, to protect the person from re-experiencing the pain. We cannot navigate around these walls unless the recipient is willing to release them and trust in Jesus for their protection instead of their walls. This can create fear and resistance, so we have to proceed gently and repeatedly encourage them to choose to defer their objections to Jesus.

So, for instance, if a child is neglected or suffers from separation, he may form the belief that loving hurts and that it is dangerous to need. As a result he may create a defense mechanism that in adult life will prevent him from getting emotionally intimate, even with his spouse. A child that suffers physical or emotional abuse may form the belief that if she does not keep everything under control, she will get hurt. Here the defense mechanism might be perfectionism, staying in control of every situation and avoiding any kind of spontaneity.

Another child who suffers a very similar kind of abuse may find a solution by vowing not to feel anymore. Here the wall serves to suppress one's emotions, resulting in a flat affect and an inability to enter into and enjoy life. In contrast, a child who grew up in a home with a dysfunctional parent (chemically addicted, emotionally ill or sickly) may form the belief, "If mother has another breakdown, everything will fall apart. If I can keep everyone happy, I'll be secure." This child's defense mechanism, then, may be to become an enabler, rescuing everyone else, which keeps others from growing and yet also wears out the enabler.

The point is that the particular solution or defense mechanism which the child adopts to deal with their childhood wounding becomes habitual. It becomes ingrained; it becomes our normality. Though it begins as just a temporary survival mechanism, in time it feels normal for us. Even if we can see how self-defeating a particular behavior or pattern is, we tend to feel that that is just the way we are and that we cannot change. This is who I am; this is just the way I was born to be. Thus as adults, even though these behavior patterns become increasingly dysfunctional and self-defeating, they are hard to break, hard to change. Our walls become our patterned, knee-jerk reaction to the experiences we encounter in the external environment in which we live.

Dissociation – Defense Mechanisms as Alters

What does the child do if he or she is too young to come up with a solution for coping with his or her pain or if the pain is too traumatic and chronic to deal with effectively. The answer is dissociation, a God-given ability to mentally disconnect from that which I do not want to know, feel, or experience. When the child dissociates, he creates a split or dissociative barrier within the mind that protects him from feeling the pain associated with the trauma. We all dissociate when we daydream while we are doing boring or repetitive tasks. Dissociation becomes a problem for the inner healing process when it bars access to remembering a painful memory that needs God's healing light and/or bars access to feeling the emotions locked within the memory.

Dissociation should be viewed as a continuum. At one end of the continuum we have daydreaming or highway hypnosis when our minds wander and we momentarily lose track of what is taking place in real time. It is the other end of the continuum, Dissociative Identity Disorder or DID, that clinicians normally think of when the term dissociation is used. In contrast to the temporary mental lapses associated with mowing the lawn or driving on the interstate, DID is an enduring state of reality by which the mind hides the atrocities of the person's life experiences from their outward conscious awareness.

Dissociation in the form of DID occurs at the time of the traumatic episode. During the trauma, the conscious outside mind looks away and is protected by alters (alternative personalities) who deal with the experience. The trauma is recorded in a dissociated state in the inner mind away from the outer mind. Dissociation suppresses and buries the emotional pain. With the passing of time, the memory becomes repressed and is no longer accessible to the conscious mind.

It is estimated that only about 1% of the population will have symptoms of DID at some point in their lifetimes. While this is, then, a fairly limited condition, it is useful to identify some of its key elements, because with DID we see in sharper form two problems that we all share in some manner.[2]

The Wounded Child – With DID, the presenting person or **host** has no awareness of or ability to access the traumatic memory. That memory and the pain associated with it is held by the originally wounded child who is walled off in the memory. This wounded child, who is variously referred to as a "little one," "authentic child" or "inner child," is a fragmented sliver or part of the person's soul. The wounded child is the actual child who went through

---

[2] The main purpose of sharing these principles is to help individuals and prayer ministers dealing with lower levels of dissociation (described below as painful memories or ego states). For advanced DID/SRA work, we highly recommend Tom and Diane Hawkins' Restoring Shattered Lives Seminar.

the original traumatic event. This child will have the same name as the host personality and will remain at the age of the traumatic event.[3]

Alters – Outside the memory in which the wounded child is held captive is a system of alters. Alters are fragmentations of the subconscious inner mind. Alters function to both keep the memory from the conscious outer mind of the host personality and to step in and function for the host when they feel the host needs their protection. Alters are commonly called multiple personalities and they may have different names, ages, and genders than the host personality. Most importantly they have different skills and abilities and, therefore, are used in different situations. This results in **switching** from host to alter or from alter to alter as the situation is perceived to require.

Similarity One – The DID model places in sharper focus what happens to all of us when we are wounded as children. As noted above, when we as children are wounded, we do two things. First we believe a lie, which is the source of the continuing emotional pain that we live with. Second, we attempt to fix ourselves and prevent ourselves from ever having to feel that intense pain again by creating a

---

[3] One of our objectives in this piece has been to use biblical language to describe the "wounded child." In Paul's prayer for the Ephesians (Eph.3:14-19), Paul uses the term "inner being" to describe this inner part of us that must be ministered to and strengthened by the Holy Spirit so that we can grasp the fullness of God's love. So we have often referred to this fragmented part of the person's soul as the "wounded inner being child." Since "the wounded inner being child" is much too cumbersome a phrase to use at every reference, we have agreed to use the term **"wounded child."**

coping strategy, a defense mechanism. So for DID people, their defense mechanism was the creation of alters. There are milder forms of dissociation, where the defense mechanism is not the creation of alters but rather the suppression and repression of the traumatic memory and/or the pain associated with it. This non-DID dissociation is absent of the major defining characteristics of DID (an alter system, the loss of time by the host when an alter assumes control, and massive internal mental fragmentation), but the dissociated person is unable to access a traumatic memory or they remember what happened, but cannot get in touch with the emotion attached to the event.

Most of us do not experience that level of dissociation, but we employ other kinds of defense mechanisms or walls to protect ourselves from having to deal with the pain. The point is that we all create defense mechanisms.

For the DID person, the walls are not subtle, rather they are an elaborate system of alters. For others the defense mechanisms may be much more subtle, but they serve the same function – to attempt to protect us from a reoccurrence of the perceived source and cause of the painful memory.

Similarity Two – The other important similarity between DID and the kind of wounding childhood memories that we all deal with is that, just as with DID, there is a wounded child left behind in all traumatic memories. That wounded child is still carrying the pain and will carry the pain until the wound has been healed. As noted, the walls we created as children to protect ourselves from having to re-experience the pain fail us as adults, because the pain leaks out and the defense mechanisms themselves become increasingly dysfunctional. Our walls also serve to isolate and in a sense wall off the wounded child. The wounded child is a part of us that has been left behind to, in a sense, carry the pain for us.

Belief and Choice

As Ed Smith (2005) has explained, the path to healing is to bring the wounded child to Jesus and ask Jesus to speak truth to the lies the child believes are causing the emotional pain. The sticking point in this healing process is often the walls we have created. The whole purpose of the defense mechanism we created was to wall off the pain so that we would never have to re-experience it again.

Say, for instance, that you were deeply humiliated in a public situation as a small child. Your childhood solution may have been to avoid attending that specific kind of gathering again.

But if avoidance is your defense mechanism, as an adult when the pain begins to leak out, your subconscious reaction is to broaden the application of the defense to other situations in which the painful emotions re-emerge. The result can be more and more exaggerated forms of avoidance until one becomes totally people phobic.

The wounded child is held captive by his or her beliefs and choices. The beliefs are the lies the child originally believed that are the source of the ongoing pain. The choices were the decisions to originally erect and subsequently maintain our walls.

The walls are our subconscious defense shields that were originally designed to protect us from feeling the pain associated with the lies. It is the fear that tearing down the walls will leave us vulnerable and unprotected that hold the walls in place.

THE HEALING PROCESS

Vision

The process of "healing the brokenhearted and setting the captives free" requires an appropriate biblical vision. Intrinsic to this vision is what Christ called the "sum of the Law."

> *Love the Lord your God with **all your heart** and with **all your soul** and with **all your mind**...and love your neighbor as yourself.*

Matthew 22: 36-40

We cannot love the Lord our God with all of our heart, soul, and mind as long as there are fragments of our inner being that continue to be held in captivity.

Furthermore, unless we partake of the Spirit's ministry of binding up the brokenhearted, setting the captive free, strengthening and ministering to the inner man that we might fully know *"the love of Christ...the height and the depth and the width and the breadth of it, greater than anything we can ever ask for or imagine, unto all the fullness of God."*

(Ephesians 3), then we can never fully love our neighbor, or be what we're called to be in Christian community.

As long as portions of our inner being remain in captivity, then we will not be able to love, minister, or worship with the freedom that God has designed us for.

One time I was ministering to a woman who clearly exhibited signs of this deep level of brokenness. She reported the loss of time, and her consternation of apparent interactions that others reported to her, of which she had no memory. More importantly, I could visibly observe her switching from one personality to another as we discussed the healing process.

In a later session I asked her what she most wanted to accomplish in therapy. Without a moments hesitation she stated, "I want to worship God with an undivided heart," quoting from Psalm 86:

Teach me Your way, O Lord, and I will walk in Your truth; give me an undivided heart, that I may fear Your name. I will praise You, O Lord my God, with all my heart; I will glorify Your name forever.

Psalm 86: 11-12

I thought that was one of the best answers that I've ever heard. She understood that her broken-heartedness was inhibiting her from a full experience in worship and loving the Lord her God with all of her heart, soul, and mind.

This realization is not typical. In the beginning stages of healing the brokenhearted, it's not unusual for the ministry recipient to have no clue as to his or her true condition of brokenness. It's all that person has ever known. We typically do not know how bound we are until we begin to agree with Christ's ministry of setting the captive free. David expressed something of this heart condition this way:

Surely you desire truth in the inner parts. You teach me wisdom in the inmost places...Create in me a clean heart O God, and renew a right spirit within me.

Psalm 51:6,10

Suffering

Another important biblical application to this ministry is that of suffering. I think it's safe to say that in our culture we do everything humanly possible to avoid a life of suffering, believe we are entitled to a pain-free life, and very often think something is horribly wrong if we suffer at all. This attitude is very different from a biblical perspective.

When I first engaged in my own healing process, I was so angry that my dialogue with God for the first couple of weeks sounded something like, "Why God...why...why did You let that happen to me...don't You take any better care of your kids than this...why God...why?" This dialogue was much more elaborate, but expressed the same sentiment in a number of different ways.

Finally, one morning I was at it again, when in the midst of my railing I paused for a breath. At this point, the still small voice of the Lord came. In the most loving and compassionate tone that you can imagine, He said, "Andy, you can continue to scream 'why,' or you can enter into the healing provision that I've made for you. The choice is yours."

I was stunned, but with considerable meditation on what had just happened, I came to understand that not only is the healing of the brokenhearted a primary mission of Christ, but agreeing with this ministry in my life is an act of obedience. During this time, He directed me to a couple of related passages.

During the days of Jesus' life on earth, He offered up prayers and petitions with loud cries and tears to the one who could save Him from death, and He was heard because of His reverent submission. Although He was a son, He learned obedience from what He suffered...

Hebrews 5:7-8

*The Spirit himself testifies with our spirit that we are God's children. Now if we are children, then we are heirs—heirs of God and co-heirs with Christ, **if indeed we share in His sufferings** in order that we may also share in His glory.*

Romans 8:16-17

Most of us like the sound of the "glory" part, but we must **share** in his sufferings **in order** that we may also share in his glory. Those of you who have experienced the restorative ministry of healing your broken heart understand that embracing your suffering with Christ leads to glory! In resolving past

130

trauma with its accompanying lies, it is important to realize the truth that entering this healing process requires that you **share** in His sufferings.

Isaiah 53 makes it clear that Jesus bought our suffering. He owns it. We never have to deal with that suffering alone. We may have to revisit it to get resolution and see the captivity of that part of our heart freed, but we must understand that we can only do so in the context of sharing the sufferings of Christ. He bought our suffering and in this process, I like to say, "Now He's come to collect what He already owns."

Three Kinds of Brokenheartedness

Any understanding of "brokenheartedness" from a clinical perspective must refer back to the continuum of dissociation. We've already alluded to the fact that brokenheartedness, (some form of dissociation with its accompanying features) can occur to varying degrees along the traumatic continuum of dissociation. As the level of trauma increases along this continuum, there is an increasing need for what Ed Smith calls an amnesic barrier between the inner mind reality and the outer mind reality.

In any case, the mind found it necessary to separate the painful inner mind reality from the outer mind reality, so that the individual could somehow store in captivity the painful memory and concurrently continue with the normal functioning of life.

While dissociation allowed the child to survive, it leads to increasing dysfunctionality in adulthood, until such time as the individual's will comes into agreement with the Spirit's intercession (Romans 8). This is the work of setting the captivity free (Isaiah 61), so that *"out of (the Father's) glorious riches He may strengthen you with power through His Spirit in* your inner being (Ephesians 3:14-21).

As we've already discussed, all people do low-level dissociating, such as daydreaming or highway hypnosis. This type of dissociation can occur only when the activity being carried out by the body is so familiar that the brain has been programmed to carry it out automatically without the direction of the mind. This form is minimally disruptive to normal functioning (Hawkins, 2006, p5)

For the purposes of this discussion, I would like to recognize three different degrees of painful inner mind reality that I commonly see in the counseling setting. From the lowest degree of dissociation on up, there is the typical painful memory, followed by a mid-range form of dissociation that I refer to as "ego states." And finally, at the most extreme level, DID. All three states have some form of the wounded inner being child.

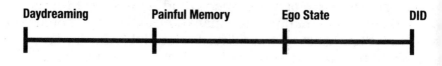

Daydreaming **Painful Memory** **Ego State** **DID**

FIGURE 1 - THE CONTINUUM OF DISSOCIATION

In the painful memory, it may be just some past painful memory of the individual at a younger time, containing its inherent lie or lies, and trauma. I have defined trauma as an overwhelming painful event that is stuck in time and space. Trauma is stored in the raw data forms of flooding emotion and body memory, just as it was received through the five senses. When accessed, the trauma event feels as though it is still happening in the present. I have observed that trauma can be experienced in conjunction with any of the three dissociative forms that I am referring to.

In the next form of dissociation, an ego state is formed when the pain of the experience is sufficiently more intense, requiring a further delineation in the painful inner mind reality. With an ego state, the wounded inner being child is experienced as the same age of the child that experienced the original trauma, or as a representative age, if the theme of trauma was consistent over a period of time.

Just as in a painful memory, the visually gifted person may see and experience this child and his or her emotional pain, but finds that the ego state form is more personified than the child in a painful memory. When accessed, the person knows what the ego state is feeling and thinking which reflects a greater degree of co-presence than more severe forms of dissociation, such as in DID. A good example of an ego state would be Kathi's description of "Fat Kathi."

With DID (as already discussed) there is an even sharper delineation between the inner mind reality and the outer mind reality. In the inner mind reality we find alters blocking access to the traumatic memories which hold the wounded children. Alters are even more personified and actually have their own voice and opinions about things. Although alters are a fragmented part of the person, they are experienced as separate personalities.[4]

The Brokenhearted Model

I like to create visuals for the individuals that I work with. Some people are auditory learners and some are visual learners. People who struggle with dissociation seem to be very visually oriented and tend to benefit greatly from these truths being taught in a visual manner. I keep a dry eraser board in my office and typically share the following model with people who are resolving a single traumatic memory, ego states, or alter personalities. The drawing is altered to fit the appropriate scenario.

In Figure 2, the complete heart represents a person's entire soul. While the composition of man's being may be debated, my sense is that since we are created in God's image, and He is a Trinity that lives in unbroken communion between Father, Son, and Holy Spirit—then we are most likely a tripartite creation, meant to live in open communion between

---

[4] These observations regarding varying degrees of dissociation are consistent with those found in research which describes how the brain responds to increasing levels of trauma. Ellert Nijenhuis, Otto van der hart, and Kathy Steele describe three levels of dissociation: primary, secondary and tertiary dissociation. (cited in Hawkins, 2006, p50-52)

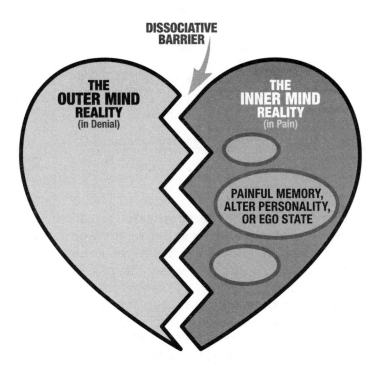

FIGURE 2 – THE BROKEN HEART

body, soul, and spirit, as well as in extended communion to the greater body of Christ. Nevertheless, our captivity seems to exist in the realm of the soul – the emotions (the broken heart) the mind (beliefs) and the will (choice).

The left half of the heart represents the **outer mind reality** that lives in some degree of denial about the **inner mind reality**, depicted by the right side of the heart. I don't view this state of denial as dysfunctional, but on the contrary, view it as the way we continue to grow and function in life, despite the painful memories, false beliefs and trauma that are held in captivity in the inner mind reality.

The **crack** separating the two halves of the heart is representative of the **amnesic or dissociative barrier** between the inner mind reality and the outer mind reality. It could also be representative of the outer and inner walls previously discussed. Whatever form this barrier takes, it isolates the painful inner being mind reality from the outer mind reality.

The **circles** on the right represent some form of painful memory with its inherent lies. As discussed previously, these forms most often refer to an isolated painful memory or memories, ego states, or with DID, alter personalities. In the case of a simple painful memory, one circle represents a single painful memory, with additional circles representing other painful memories. A circle might also represent an ego state or alter personality, with additional circles representing additional ego states or alter personalities.

As previously discussed, Dr. Ed Smith argues that a painful memory is a container for lies. We are not in emotional pain because of what happened to us, but because of the painful lies that we associate with our interpretation of the event. For example, if I were sexually molested I might believe that I'm dirty and shameful, that I'm not wanted or loved, or that all I'm good for is to be used.

These beliefs do not agree with the cognitive Christian truth that we have assimilated into other parts of our mind and being, but truth must be received at the point of infection. This ministry is very site specific–meaning God's truth must be encountered at the specific site where some form of brokenness is held captive. I often make this point by saying, "If I have a splinter in my finger, the solution is not to amputate my foot."

Without understanding what we were doing, in our attempts to help, we in the church have often applied truth to the wrong place in the soul. To spout Christian truth in a shotgun fashion accomplishes nothing except, perhaps, when the person finds no freedom after this form of ministry, establishes further possible falsehoods that "I must be the only one for whom this will not work", "I must be unacceptable to God", "God doesn't want to set me free", or "I must have some hidden sin that is preventing me from receiving from God." The list of wrong conclusions could go on and on.[5]

---

[5] This does not dismiss conviction of sin, which is always part of the healing/sanctification process.

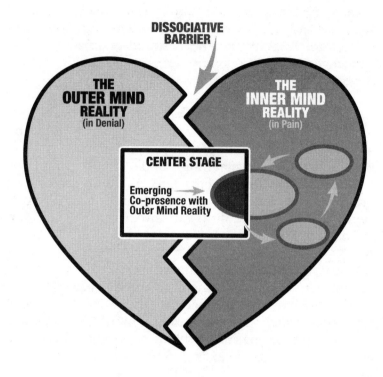

FIGURE 3 – THE CENTER STAGE

The place of site-specific ministry or what I like to call "**center stage**" is depicted in Figure 3 by the rectangle in the middle of the broken heart. This stage bridges the chasm or dissociative barrier between the painful inner mind reality and the denial outer mind reality. The outer mind reality comes to this stage, in agreement with the leading of the Holy Spirit, to reconcile with the inner being child, validates the child's pain and function, participates in feeling and defining the child's lies, and agrees as the Holy Spirit of Christ replaces this falsehood with the truth that sets us free. (John 8:31-32, 36; 14:15-16, 25; 16:13-15).

I believe that the Holy Spirit makes intercession for the wounded child to be revealed to the outer mind reality, *"with groans too deep for words"* (Romans 8:26-27), and is the agent which continues Christ's primary mission of *"healing the broken-hearted and setting the captives free."*

Knowing this truth, it is imperative that the person's outer mind reality willfully choose to come into agreement with this intercession of the Holy Spirit.

In all the years that I have witnessed this kind of healing, I have not once witnessed the Spirit of Christ violating the will of an individual in order to accomplish His intercession. If the person is not ready, He simply allows them to go around the mountain one more time till such time as he is ready. I am reasonably convinced that God, in His sovereignty, uses and orchestrates circumstances and events so that all things would work together for good.

It is our hope that this teaching will reduce the number of trips we must take around the mountain in pursuit of true healing—what Kathi likes to call "the real deal."

There are a couple of ways that this transaction can happen. In the case of Kathi Oates' ministry, she actively sets the stage in agreement with the Spirit's intercession for the wounded child parts to be revealed and made known (come center stage). The beauty of this model is that the individual, already in an anointed setting, is free to see and work with any wounded children that are revealed, without a traumatic triggering event, which more often clues us into the presence of a wounded child.

Outside of a proactive ministry setting, such as Gary's and Kathi's meetings, most individuals encounter a painful inner being part of themselves when some life event triggers it onto center stage.

An example of this might be Mary who experienced significant inner panic every time her husband had to leave town on a business trip. We used this emotion, tracking it to get in touch with an inner being child place that was abandoned by her father at two years of age.

Once a circle begins to come center stage, if we don't understand what the Holy Spirit is trying to accomplish, we often respond by exerting energy to keep it off of center stage. This is depicted by the circle, halfway on stage. The barred area shows that the painful inner being reality is becoming co-present with the outer mind reality.

The curved arrows demonstrates a painful inner being reality that is not allowed to come fully co-present with the outer mind reality. It is simply relegated back to its place in the inner mind reality, only to reemerge at a later time. We might respond by exerting energy to keep this inner being part off center stage for a number of reasons:

1. The wounded child is accompanied by painful emotion that we don't like feeling.

2. Sometimes the wounded child will share haunting images of abuse, or an extremely unnerving image.

   Jane came to me expressing shame that for much of her adult Christian life, when she talked to a man, she would often see a phallic image in her mind. She had fasted, prayed, undergone deliverance ministry, but the image persisted over years. Instead of pushing the image away, we agreed to ask the Holy Spirit to show her what inner being part of her was sharing this image. She immediately went to a 4 year old memory where a teenage boy who was a friend of the family locked her in the bathroom with him, exposed himself to her and invited her to touch his genitals. In ministry, this inner being child was eager to be reconciled to the adult outer mind reality, and quickly allowed Jesus to take the trauma. The plaguing phallic image has never returned.

3. The wounded child always holds beliefs that we defend against. I previously gave the example of the abuse victim who believed at the inner being level that he was dirty, wasn't worth protecting, and was only good for being used. These deep inner beliefs are so painful to feel that we often defend and fight against them by not allowing the inner being child who presents with them to come center stage.

It is not unusual for individuals to describe manifestations of inner being pain as an attack of the enemy or a demonic infestation that requires deliverance. The irony of this interpretation is that it is the intercession of the Holy Spirit which is prompting the wounded child to come front and center so that captivity can be set free and the individual can participate in a greater sanctification of their soul.

A further irony is that without this under-standing, subjecting the wounded child to deliverance ministry often results in a deeper traumatization of the wounded child locked in the painful memory. It is not unusual for wounded children to have demonic attachments, but they leave quietly once the foothold of deceiving lies is replaced with Holy Spirit truth in a very peaceful process.

Ministering to Walls

As we move down the dissociative continuum, we come to the more common range of simple painful memories.   At this level, what we mean by dissociation is any means by which we distance the outer conscious self from the pain the wounded child is holding in the memory. Often these are the walls or defense mechanisms we have discussed above.

It is these walls that often prevent a painful memory from coming center stage. The walls were originally designed to defend ourselves against having to re-experience the pain of the initial traumatic memory. They have been working hard at trying to accomplishing that purpose, perhaps for decades. Even when the pain begins leaking out and they become increasingly dysfunctional in our lives, at the subconscious level, part of us believes that they are serving a vital function and that their removal could subject us to overwhelming pain. It is this fear that typically pushes memories back into the subconscious inner mind as they begin to come center stage.

It is these milder forms of dissociation that we deal with in the vast majority of cases. Often a prayer recipient will have difficulty either accessing a memory or getting in touch with the emotion held in the memory.

As they approach a memory, everything may go black or they may sense some kind of barrier preventing them from accessing the memory. More commonly, their defense mechanisms unconsciously come forward to protect them from making direct contact with negative memories and negative emotions.

If they can see a wall blocking access to a wounded child, I might ask them if the wall has a name. Typically the name is its function. Common examples are isolation, perfectionism, or control.

I often ask how this wall is protecting the person and instruct the person to pay attention to any impressions or inner voices. I then ask the wall if it is willing to meet Jesus (as one might do with an alter). If they are willing to speak with Jesus, He will generally calm their fears so that they are willing to step aside and allow Jesus to minister to the wounded child.

For prayer recipients who are not so visual and can't see or sense a wall, I might ask them what would happen if you really got in contact with the memory and felt the painful emotions held in it. Examples of typical responses include things like, "I think I'll die," "I won't be able to bear the pain," or "I'll lose my family."

The answer to that question is usually what Ed Smith calls a guardian lie. When that lie is referred to Jesus and He speaks His truth, the prayer recipient is usually willing to move forward and access the painful memory.

Then following TPM principles, the painful emotions the wounded child is holding in the memory are used to identify the lie and I ask Jesus to speak His truth into that wounded child place.

Reconciliation with the Wounded Child

Because of the wall or dissociative barrier between the inner being mind reality and the outer mind reality, there often exists tremendous conflict between these two parts. The conscious mind has been in denial of the inner being state to the point of disowning or rejecting the wounded child.

This conflict requires some form of biblical reconciliation. I cannot stress enough the importance of the outer mind reality making a choice of the will to fully engage the inner mind reality and the pain that the wounded child is holding.

All forms of the wounded child (those held captive in painful memories, ego states and alter personalities or authentic children), often feel completely ignored, abandoned, and unappreciated for how he or she has helped the outer mind reality in containing the painful trauma and beliefs related to the painful incident.

This conflict is more pronounced the further one goes up the dissociative ladder towards advanced DID. This part of a person will often complain that not only has the outer mind reality refused to acknowledge the trauma that he or she has contained for so many years, but has genuinely been mistreated and hated for daring to suggest to the outer mind reality that the inner pain is true and real.

Likewise, the outer mind reality often feels very real derision for the inner mind reality. On more than one occasion, I have had this person say, "I just wish that I could lop this part off of me!" This attitude requires genuine repentance that can best be achieved through a reconciliation process.

Years ago, I would invite both mind realities to stay present and share their respective perceived truths. The inner being mind reality would express anger over being ignored and having been relegated to a pain-filled existence. There usually is more required of the outer mind reality in coming to acceptance of the inner being reality. I would work to help each respectfully see the other's perspective and role until there was relative acceptance between the two.

While I understood this need for reconciliation for many years, I am extremely grateful to Dr. Bill Tollefson for enumerating several key points of this reconciliation in his book, *Separated From The Light*, as well as several clients that have clarified and added content to these points based on the unique needs of their own therapy. I haven taken the liberty to plainly incorporate biblical truth within this reconciliation script.

In this process, the outer mind reality must be willing to seek reconciliation with the inner mind reality. When using this script, give both the outer and inner mind realities permission to stop and clarify any point that may be giving them trouble.

You should have a general sense of peace if the reconciliation is proceeding nicely. Since denial is a major role of the outer mind reality, it's not unusual for this individual to "numb out" during key features of the reconciliation that cause him or her to engage in the inner being reality's pain. When this happens, I simply ask that the outer mind reality stay engaged, using Theophostic prayer as needed to make it safe for the outer mind reality to do so.

What follows is a vignette that uses these re-conciliation principles. Please keep in mind that this has been used successfully hundreds of times, regardless of the form of dissociation.

Using the Reconciliation Script

I previously mentioned the case of Jane, who came to me expressing shame, that for much of her life, when she engaged in conversation with men, a phallic image would invade her mind. Despite fasting and prayer, binding and undergoing deliverance ministry, the image persisted. We discussed the possibility that a wounded inner being child might be presenting itself for ministry and Jane agreed to ask the Holy Spirit to show her if this were so.

She immediately recalled a memory where of herself as a four-year-old where a teenage boy had exposed himself to her, inviting her to touch his genitalia. As she recalled this memory, she relived the confusion, shame, and fear of the moment. I asked Jane if she were willing to let me lead her through reconciliation with this long-neglected wounded child. She was willing and the reconciliation followed something like this:

"Jane, is it alright if we call this inner being child Little Jane?" She responded that it would be. I explained that I was going to lead her through a reconciliation with Little Jane, and to please let me know if she was having difficulty at any juncture.

"I want you to focus again on what Little Jane is feeling." Jane quickly reported that she was very co-present with Little Jane, could see Jesus holding her, and was ready to speak to her.

"Good. Now I'd like you to repeat what I say. (Have the person repeat line by line). Little Jane, I'm sorry that we ever had to be split apart and that you were left there to deal with situations that were too overwhelming, frightening, and painful. I didn't really mean to leave you. It just happened. But it was the only way that we could survive. Please forgive me for leaving you there. I realize now that you are not to blame for what happened. We were just a child and no child could be responsible for such a thing. But thank you for holding this pain all these years." Tears began streaming down Jane's face.

I continued sentence by sentence or phrase by phrase with Jane repeating after me, "I've come with Jesus today to rescue you from this painful existence. I don't want to live with a divided heart and I need you to be with me. I want you to come and be reunited with me in a place where you can be free from all the past pain, hurt, fear, and trauma— where you will be free to be whole, healthy and happy, free to grow with Jesus for the first time in your life."

I then entered the promise phase of the reconciliation which focuses on issues of how we blame and shame our wounded child parts, how we have dismissed their presenting feelings, as well as the issue of abandonment for having been left.

I continued, "Little Jane, if you choose to come be reunited with me, I promise not to blame or shame you, and I'm sorry for the way that I've done that. I promise not to dismiss or minimize your feelings, and I'm sorry for the way that I've done that."

Jane began weeping and exclaimed, "I'm so very sorry. I didn't understand and so I hated you. Please forgive me!" I paused allowing Jane time to process this, then continued with Jane repeating the words, "Little Jane, more than anything, I want you to know that I will never leave or abandon you again—so help me God. And if in some way I do distance from you, with the Holy Spirit's help, I will be quick to repent."

We paused to let this sink in, then continued, "Little Jane, I again want to thank you for holding this pain all these years—for doing for me what I could not do for myself. You actually have been very courageous, brave, and strong. I'm proud of you and I love you."

Jane smiled through her tears, reporting, "She's smiling and holding my hand."

The Importance of Releasing Trauma

Following the reconciliation, I asked Jane to stay engaged, by maintaining eye contact with Little Jane. Then I instructed her that in accordance with Isaiah 61, we were going to pray that the prison door would be opened (to the trauma of the wounded child) and that this captivity would be set free, inviting the trauma to flow to Jesus. As the trauma dumped out and flowed to Jesus, I prayed excerpts of Isaiah 53. It sounded something like this:

"Lord Jesus, we now agree with the intercession of Your Spirit that the prison door to Little Jane's heart would be open and that all the hurt, pain, emotion and body memory will flow to You. So even as we pray right now, with the prison door open, we pray that it all would begin dumping and flowing to You...dumping...dumping...dumping...flowing....flowing... flowing, all the pain flowing to Jesus. As Your Word says, 'You were wounded for all the transgression against her...You were bruised for all the iniquity against her...surely You bore and are bearing all her grief and sorrows...and by Your stripes she is healed.' For You said, 'Come unto me all you who are heavy-laden and I will give you rest.' Flowing...flowing...flowing, all the heaviness, pain and trauma flowing to Jesus."

I continued praying in this fashion until Jane indicated the trauma had stopped flowing. If it takes several minutes, I'll ask every few minutes if the trauma is still flowing. If it is, I simply continue praying in the same fashion till it stops.

Some individuals report this trauma appearing to exit like fast speed videotape. Others report it sounding like a rushing wind. Still others report a progressive release of a feeling of heaviness until it is all gone.[6]

---

[6] Counselors and prayer ministers alike may hear the details of so much abuse and trauma that they can be traumatized. This "secondary abuse or trauma" has been well documented in the literature. While it is a privilege to share in the sufferings of Christ, the prayer minister wasn't created to perpetually carry this pain either. My habit is to periodically release or dump this secondary trauma in the same way the prayer recipient is doing. This often happens while the recipient is releasing trauma.

With the trauma gone, it's much easier for the child to receive Holy Spirit truth to replace the false beliefs that came with the wounding. We use Theophostic Prayer Ministry to ensure that this happens. I typically work with the wounded child's emotion before the reconciliation and release of trauma to get a clear picture of the false beliefs the child is holding. It is preferable for the child to receive truth before the reconciliation process. Occasionally, the wounded child is so deeply triggered in trauma that she is unable to focus on any ministry (reconciliation or identifying false beliefs). This will manifest as extreme agitation with an inability to focus. When this happens, it is highly beneficial to get some release from the trauma first. Simply instruct the individual what you believe is happening and how you will pray for the release of trauma.

Figure 4 depicts the release of trauma, site-specific truth being received by the wounded child, as well as the captive set free. Once the reconciliation and subsequent release of trauma is achieved, I then go back to see if all the false beliefs have been replaced with Holy Spirit truth.

I leave it to Jesus to let the outer mind reality know what portion of the suffering he wants him or her to embrace. I agree with Dr. Tollefson who believes that it is not necessary for the individual to re-experience the trauma, since they have already lived through it once.

This differs from Dr. Smith's belief that all the emotional pain has to be embraced, but I reason that Jesus won't lead astray and since He purchased the

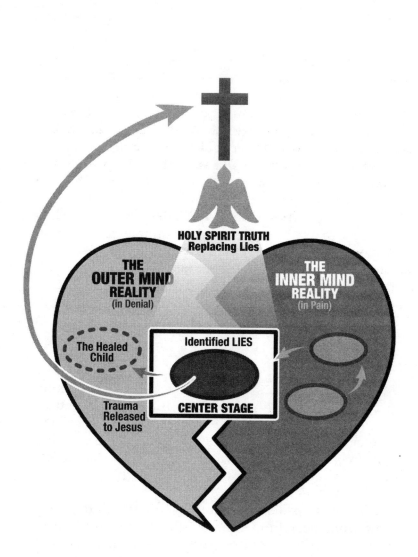

FIGURE 4 – FULL CO-PRESENCE, RELEASING TRAUMA, RECEIVING TRUTH, THE CAPTIVE SET FREE.

pain, it's His to do with as He sees fit. Having said this, it's not unusual for the outer mind reality to get the full impact of specific traumas, complete with abreaction (a flooding of emotional and body memory). This trauma typically releases very quickly and in the presence of Jesus, complete peace will come.

The Captives Set Free

Once the wounded child has received truth to replace the lies, has been reconciled to the outer person, and been released of trauma, the child is free to leave the inner prison of captivity. At this point in the ministry, there is usually a sharing of tears between the inner being child and the outer mind reality.

I almost always ask Jesus if He is willing to bless the child and "restore all that the locusts have eaten away." He always seems eager to do so. We then pray for an infilling of His Spirit in this place that has only known pain. With Jane, it sounded something like this:

"Jane, God's Word states that the power of the Holy Spirit strengthens and ministers to your inner being so that you might know the height and the depth and the width and the breadth of the love of Christ, greater than anything you could ever ask or imagine, unto all the fullness of God. Would it be alright if we prayed for this fullness?" Jane responded that it would be.

"Okay then, Lord Jesus, we ask You to fill all that has been vacated with the presence of Your Spirit...filling...filling...filling...unto all the fullness of God...we pray that rivers of living water would rush up and in...flowing...flowing...flowing. We simply continue praying this way until the individual indicates filling has stopped and she's very full. I like to pause and really let the recipient enjoy this time with the Lord.

I often invite the outer person if he or she wants to hug the inner person. If either part is reluctant, there may be more work to do. More often, he or she is ready to do so, and there's a joyful reunion. Some times this hug will result in the spontaneous fusion of the inner child into the person. Other times, Jesus will escort them to a pain-free safe place, as is more typical with DID. Either way, the person should be experiencing perfect peace.

Figure 4 also shows the child state living in barrier-free communion with the outer mind reality, as depicted by the dotted circular line.

Of course, it is so wonderful to see the ministry many individuals are free to move in once they no longer have to spend huge amounts of energy protecting their pain. It should be noted, however, most individuals have the need to do a number of healing pieces before entering this kind of freedom.

But once these principles are learned, they can easily become incorporated into your spiritual dis-cipline and used whenever you are triggered in some past pain. These principles are becoming such a fixed part of our healing community, so that just as they did with Gary and Kathi, when one of us is triggered, it is an easy matter to get it resolved quickly.

Kathi's Pioneering Work

We view the work that Kathi has been doing in the context of conference and overseas crusade ministry sessions as path breaking. What you have been reading in this book is the product of Kathi's own search for inner healing, as well as her pioneering efforts to apply what she has learned to a mass setting under the unction of the Holy Spirit. We believe that Kathi's work holds a unique relevance for our time for three reasons.

(1) The Lessons of History – There is a stream of thought in the Christian community that believes that all of our past sins, wrong choices, and emotional wounds were fully redeemed when we came to the Cross and gave our lives to Jesus. Kathi is leading a bold assault against this view. There is nothing in the Bible that suggests that we become a sanctified, pure, and spotless bride at the moment of baptism. As Kathi has pointed out, history is littered with many powerful ministries that ultimately crashed and burned because of character flaws in the leadership.

Time is short. The Church can no longer afford the luxury of ignoring the issues of inner healing. Satan can only attack us where there are chinks or gaps in our spiritual armor. He knows exactly where those places of vulnerability are in each of us. These are the places where we believe lies and/or where we created defense mechanisms.

Our self-made childhood solutions designed to protect us from pain, as adults have become increasingly dysfunctional walls that lock us into behavior patterns that are fouling our relationships and denying us ability to walk in the fullness and freedom that God has intended for us. Our lies and walls are points of attack that Satan can use to render our work for God's kingdom ineffective and bring us down. If we are going to avoid the failures of the past, the Church, and especially the Church leadership, must take seriously the work of inner healing.

(2) Modeling the Path – Kathi's work is exceptionally courageous because she not only talks about the need for inner healing in the Church, but she reveals the details of her own struggle. This is a brave thing to do, because there is a spirit in the Church that demands that its leaders be perfect. Leaders must always project a façade of strength, because if they were to reveal the internal emotional turmoil they are really experiencing, they would be abandoned. As long as Jesus' message stuck to the themes of the Kingdom of God has come and healing, He attracted massive followings. When He started talking about suffering and death, the crowds left.

What makes Kathi's ministry so relevant is that the path she has modeled is not only needed in the leadership. There is a transition coming in the Church which will finally witness Luther's principle of the priesthood of all believers. Gone are the days of the spectator Church, where a few generals led the way and everyone else just followed.

The next move of God will be led by a massive nameless, faceless generation of sergeants from all walks of life. All of us who want to enter in and stay the course for the coming great move of God will need to have dealt with their inner healing issues.

(3) Doing the Stuff – Kathi is not only sounding the alarm and modeling what we all need to do. Real major inner healing breakthroughs are occurring in her meetings. How can this be? All of the major approaches and models of inner healing suggest that this work can only be done through a multitude of sessions with a Christian counselor or lay ministry team over an extended period of time. Ed Smith does not even endorse one-on-one telephone ministry as an effective and valid means of inner healing.

In one regard, it is certainly true that the deeper the wounding, generally the longer the healing process takes. Moreover, inner healing is a lifelong process in the sense that we will never be completely healed of all our lies and walls until we see Jesus face to face. Yet, we can gain freedom from the big debilitating issues that mess up our lives. But how can any inner healing take place in a mass setting?

A Philosophical Dilemma – On the one hand, we know that it does, on occasion, spontaneously happen from reports from the Toronto Airport Christian Fellowship and elsewhere, where it has been found that a number of people who have rested in the Spirit at their meetings have had an encounter with God. People sometimes emerge from this "carpet time" changed, sometimes through a physical healing and sometimes through an inner healing.

That phenomenon has been viewed as a sovereign act of God. People fall out under the Spirit and God sometimes chooses to act in profound ways. It is quite a different matter to lead a mass session in inner healing with the expectation that many people are going to receive a significant healing.

Here, we are bumping up against an age-old philosophical issue that has engaged theologians for centuries. As the 19th century Christian existentialist philosopher Soren Kierkegaard put it, "God is in control of all things, but I must choose." The omnipotence of God and the free will of man seem to collide. How can both be true? Many have resolved this dilemma by arguing that God chooses to not violate our willful choices because He wants us to freely choose Him.

Why Does It Work? – If that is true, where does that leave us in regard to the possibility of mass inner healing? God may choose to occasionally violate our choices and breach the walls we have erected to bring healing to our broken hearts. But with mass healings in a mass setting, that explanation fails. Rather than just conclude that God works in mysterious ways, let us suggest an explanation that does not do violence to the concept of man's free will and the importance of our choices in the healing process.

We have chosen to rely on our own solutions, our self-created defense mechanisms to protect us from the pain of emotional woundings. What was once a desperate choice by a child trying to cope with some overwhelming pain and just survive, has become a subconscious knee-jerk response.

No matter how dysfunctional our walls have become, we cling to them and fear letting them go, because of the belief that they are our only protection and that we will be completely vulnerable without them. Our mind knows that "God will supply all of our needs," but our heart does not trust Him. According to the wounded child's perception, He was not there during the original traumatic event and so He still cannot be trusted to protect us now.

As we have noted, this is often a sticking point in counseling or lay ministry settings. These sub-conscious fears in the child's heart inhibit and delay progress toward walking in greater freedom.

Could it be that the results that Kathi is seeing in her mass ministry sessions flow from the effect the heavy presence of the Lord has on silencing our subconscious internal objections to trusting Him? Under the anointing, it is simply easier to choose to trust Jesus.

When we are experientially overwhelmed by the presence of God and can feel His waves of love and peace flowing through our bodies, our walls fall down. In that atmosphere it is suddenly and vividly obvious to many that we don't need to protect ourselves.

God powerfully shows up and our rebellious, questioning, doubting, self-protecting spirit is silenced. The God we have always sought, the God we have yearned for, our loving, compassionate, protecting champion, our El Shadai is here and we freely give Him access to the deepest recesses of our hearts to do His healing work.

The Task Before Us – Perhaps you have noticed that it is hard to find spotless brides in the Church that are prepared for Jesus' return. There is a staggering amount of sanctifying, inner healing work that remains to be done, both within the present Church and among the masses of new converts that will soon be piling into the Church. The prophets are telling us to expect one billion converts in a new healing revival that is rapidly coming upon the church. We need a miracle in the area of inner healing to get the Church where it needs to be.

Bless you, Kathi for pioneering this great work!

Appendix B

SUGGESTED READINGS

For those who want to dig deeper into the inner healing process, the place to begin is with Theophostic Prayer Ministry, as outlined in Ed Smith's introductory book, *Healing Life's Hurts through Theophostic Prayer* (Regal, Ventura, CA, 2002) or his major text *Theophostic Prayer Ministry: Basic Seminar Manual* (New Creation Publishing, Campbellsville, KY, 2005).

For a more general understanding of inner healing principles see Mary Pitches, *Set My People Free; Yesterday's Child; and Dying to Change* (Hodder and Stoughton, London, 1987, 1990, 1996), Chester and Betsy Kylstra, *Restoring the Foundations: Counseling by the Living Word* (Proclaiming His Word, 1996) and the large number of pioneering works by John and Paula Sandford, including *The Transformation of the Inner Man* (Bridge Publishing, Plainfield, NJ, 1982) and *Healing the Wounded Spirit* (Victory House, Tulsa, OK, 1985).

Also useful are Christian Healing Ministry's *School of Healing Prayer* (Jacksonville, FL), Michael Evans, *Learning to Do What Jesus Did* (Archer-Ellison, Winter Park, FL 1996) and the work by Neil Anderson, including *The Steps to Freedom in Christ* (Gospel Light, 2004).

For work focused on Dissociative Identity Disorder and healing from severe psychological trauma see Terri A. Clark, *More Than One: An Inside Look at Multiple Personality Disorder* (Thomas Nelson, Nashville, 1993), Tom and Diane Hawkins, *Restoring Shattered Lives Seminar* (Restoration in Christ Ministries, Grottoes, VA, 2006), William B. Tollefson, *Separated from the Light: a Path Back from Psychological Trauma* (Tollefson Enterprises, Cape Coral, FL, 1997), and James Friesen, *Uncovering the Mystery of MPD* (Here's Life Publishers, San Bernardino, CA, 1991).

For a model of healing in the church community, see Jim Wilder et al., *The Life Model: Living from the Heart Jesus Gave You* (Shepherd's House, Pasadena, CA, 2004).

Appendix C

GLOSSARY[7]

Alter – Abbreviated form of "alternative personality;" an alternative or separate personality that exits in the mind of a person with Dissociative Identify Disorder.

Amnesic or Dissociative Barrier – A wall of denial between the conscious and subconscious minds. The barrier between the conscious (outer mind reality) and subconscious (inner mind reality) mind, such that the conscious mind is protected from and rendered incapable or accessing one or more painful memories stored in the subconscious.

Body Memory – The re-experiencing of the physical sensations of a past event.

Coconsciousness or Copresence – Referring to varying degrees to which one alter can know the thoughts of another alter or the host or where parts of the inner mind reality can

---

[7] While these definitions are widely accepted in the literature, we borrowed heavily from the glossaries found in the works by Hawkins and Clark, cited above.

communicate with and be present with the outer mind reality.

Dissociation – A defense mechanism that operates unconsciously wherein the mind blocks out conscious memory and awareness of either present events while the mind is preoccupied elsewhere or of a painful past memory that it does not want to recall.

Dissociative Identity Disorder (DID) – The new official term for what was formerly know as Multiple Personality Disorder (MPD); the presence of two or more distinct personalities or personality states within a single person, two or more of which recurrently take control of the individual's behavior.

Host Personality – In DID the presenting personality who has executive control of the body the majority of the time.

Integration – The process of bringing together alters or ego states so that only one integrated personality exists.

Splinter/Part/Fragment – These terms can refer to a wounded child, ego state, or alter that is dissociated from the conscious mind.

Splitting/Fracture – The process of dissociation in which an alter or ego state is formed.

Switching – In DID, moving from the conscious awareness of the host to an alter state of consciousness; the process of changing executive control of the body from one alter-identity to another.

Trauma – An overwhelming painful event that is stuck in time and space such that the event is stored in the raw data forms of flooding emotion and body memory, just as it was originally received through the five senses.

Trigger – A particular stimulus that causes a given response, as when something in a current event reminds the subconscious mind of a suppressed painful memory and causes the raw emotions stored in that memory to flood into the present consciousness, without any awareness of where the emotion is coming from.

Wall – A defense mechanism established, generally in childhood, to help the child cope with a painful event by instituting what becomes an automatic behavioral response in an attempt to protect the person from re-experiencing the pain of the initial trauma.

Wounded Child – The child who is left behind to deal with the emotional pain in any traumatic memory that has been dissociated from the conscious mind.

BIOGRAPHICAL SKETCHES

Andrew A. Miller, LCSW, has practiced as a professional individual, marriage, and family therapist for the past fifteen years. He is a graduate of Florida State University (M.S.W. 1990) where his program emphasized marriage and family treatment. While he continues working in marriage and family treatment, the bulk of his practice is focused on resolving dissociation and trauma in those suffering from abuse. Andy has striven to incorporate biblical healing principles with sound clinical practice.

In addition to his counseling practice, he is a faculty member of the Center for Biblical Studies in Tallahassee, Florida and currently serves as the director for Tallahassee Healing Prayer Ministries. He also serves on the Board of Gary Oates Ministries. Prior to his counseling career, Andrew served for five years on a church staff as a pastoral assistant where he was an intake and prayer counseling coordinator, trained and supervised prayer ministers, small group leaders, and Stephen Ministers. He continues to reside in Tallahassee, Florida with his wife, Lisa, and their son, Nathaniel.

Dr. Scott Flanagan taught full-time at Florida State University for 30 years though the year 2000 and part-time for the following five year until full retirement in 2005. Beginning in the early 1990s, he began to seek out training in a broad variety of approaches to inner healing. He has been involved as a lay minister in inner healing over the last decade and has been teaching and training prayer ministers since 1999 in church and the Center for Biblical Studies settings.

He serves on the Boards of Gary Oates Ministries and the Center for Biblical Studies (a Christian College and Seminary in Tallahassee), as well as chairing the Curriculum and Training Committee of the Tallahassee Healing Prayer Ministries. He lives in Tallahassee, Florida with his wife, Rita.

About the co-author...

ROBERT PAUL LAMB has worn a number of hats in more than 34 years of ministry including author, pastor, evangelist, prophet, preacher of the Gospel and missionary to the nations. However, he is best known for the 37 books (with some four million copies in print) written on the lives of some of God's great men and women.

He, Gary and Kathi Oates have been friends and ministerial acquaintances for more than 25 years. Prior to entering the ministry in 1972, he had spent most of his adult life in public relations and newspaper work. He and his family make their home in northwestern North Carolina.

Ministry Resources
by
Gary and Kathi Oates

DVD's

Open My Eyes, Lord
Angelic Visitations
Intimacy with God
Foundation for Healing
Pathways to Healing
Fulfill Your Destiny
Healing the Brokenhearted

CD's

Open My Eyes, Lord (2 CD set)
Healing the Brokenhearted (2 CD set)
Intimacy with God (2 CD Set)
Angelic Visitations
Access to the Miraculous
Heaven's Portals
Pathways to Healing
Fulfill Your Destiny

Quantity discounts available for books!

These and other titles available at:

www.GaryOates.com

Or, by phoning 1-336-667-2333

For book/tape/video orders,
please contact:

Open Heaven Publications
an outreach of Gary Oates Ministries, Inc.
P.O. Box 457/Moravian Falls, NC 28654 USA
336-667-2333

For more information, visit our website:

www.garyoates.com

**For Gary Oates' materials in Europe,
visit the following website:**

tp://newdayinternational.org/shop/customer/home.php?cat=93